SHUT THE DOOR ON
YESTERDAY

SHUT THE DOOR ON YESTERDAY
Copyright © 2022 by AGNES MARTIN

Published in the United States of America
ISBN   Paperback: 978-1-959761-22-8
ISBN   eBook: 978-1-959761-23-5

All rights reserved. No part of this publication may be reproduced, stored in a retrieval system or transmitted in any way by any means, electronic, mechanical, photocopy, recording or otherwise without the prior permission of the author except as provided by USA copyright law.

The opinions expressed by the author are not necessarily those of ReadersMagnet, LLC.

ReadersMagnet, LLC
10620 Treena Street, Suite 230 | San Diego, California, 92131 USA
1.619. 354. 2643 | www.readersmagnet.com

Book design copyright © 2022 by ReadersMagnet, LLC. All rights reserved.

Cover design by Ericka Obando
Interior design by Daniel Lopez

SHUT THE DOOR ON YESTERDAY

AGNES MARTIN

ReadersMagnet, LLC

CONTENTS

SHUT THE DOOR ON YESTERDAY 1
SOME 2
ALLOW 4
POEM FOR SCHOOL GRADUATION 5
SILENCE 6
SILENCE TODAY 7
SPEAKING OF MARRIAGE 45
PARADISE 54
CHRISTIANITY IS NOT A PHILOSOPHY 59
THE MISSION 83
IV CHAPTER 101
GOD CALLS ME BY MY NAME 105
III CHAPTER JUICE, COFFEE, TEA 111
THE PERSON WHOM I WAS AND
HOW I USED TO THINK 129
LESSONS FROM CHURCH WHY? 152
AND THOUGHTS 191
THE COMMUNION OF SAINTS 196
ENDNOTES 219

SHUT THE DOOR ON YESTERDAY

I've shut the door on yesterday, it sorrows and mistakes;
I've locked within its gloomy walls Past failures and heartaches
And now I throw the key away to seek another room
And furnish it with hope and smiles, And every springtime bloom.
No thought shall enter this abode That has a hint of pain,
And every malice and distrust Shall never therein reign.
I've shut the door on yesterday And thrown the key away-
Tomorrow holds no doubt for me, Since I have found today.

SOME

POETRY...

HOW I WEPT WHEN I HEARD YOUR HYMNS AND CANTICLES, BEING DEEPLY MOVED BY THE SWEET SINGING OF YOUR CHURCH. THOSE VOICES FLOWED INTO MY EARS, TRUTH FILTERED INTO MY HEART, AND FROM MY HEART SURGED WAVES OF DEVOTION. TEARS RAN DOWN, AND I WAS HAPPY

IN MY TEARS. (St. Augustine - Confessions on the singing of The Psalms)

ALLOW

Allow the dust of discord slowly sets on the bed of patience

As shining speckles quietly resting on the golden sand Waiting for their turn to be useful to nature and

History.

Allow time to heal our pale, disturbing wounds as time can be our most precious "grace"

If only we won't misuse it or abuse it or untamed it. Insane would be the healer which doesn't heal Yet allow Life to make him stay alive

As Life itself is all we get

In doing so, you'll see…As we allow, we will no sin.

everybody), turbulent relationships and frustrations of every kind. My next younger sister, single mother for many years and probably alcoholic. She had some kind of nervous breakdown and that took her to a great depression and a first contact with God while attempting to kill herself. She is now a Missionary with her husband in the USA and they are very happy serving The Church. One of her sons, the oldest, was invited with his family of 10 to go to Estonia as a Mission family to help the Church spread and announce the Good News to the people of that post-communist and undeveloped country. Next comes a brother, divorced, who left his wife for another woman after he had several affairs looking for the perfect woman. He is now in another city with a woman who is probably divorced or a widow, I am not sure. He writes and uses Facebook and I am afraid he is not happy. He also used to drink a lot and his heart is not well. He doesn't keep in touch with me anyway. The baby is another girl now in her mid-50's, many dysfunctional affairs when she was younger, also a single mother and a declared alcoholic, well declared to us not to herself. She married an alcoholic, had many problems, found God (the God of the Jews) became a widow and a few months after his death, she brought a man to live with her, kept drinking, left the Church and enjoyed herself. She keeps in touch but we don't say much to each other. After the death of our mother, she became depressed and distant but she thinks she is very happy. She seems to be a loving grandmother though she takes herself very seriously. She has 12 grandchildren. She is the one who has more grandchildren for now, and for me that is an accomplishment. I have the feeling that she will fall from her "pink cloud" any time.

    I worked as an Administrative Assistant, Personnel Secretary, Receptionist, Librarian Assistant and Bilingual Instructional Assistant and in those times, when I was an Administrative Assistant and/or a Secretary there were no computers or PC's as they're named so all our written documents, letters, memorandums, etc., had to be typed and perfectly because not only we have no Word Processors but we couldn't erase or correct mistakes and anything typed on a regular typewriter has to have no errors so it would take me a long time to finish anything which was to be typed. Later on, the Market started to sell those white liquids which had to be applied very carefully because the liquid was very thick and it dried up quickly. I've also used those white rectangular pieces of special labels that look alike which you would apply in front of the letter, type and the error would be erased. It was a complicated system and it would take forever to finish a typing job. Finally, the last eraser which I've used were those tiny devices filled with erasing narrow strips of white paper which were applied while taking the document off the typewriter, covering the error and putting it back to be finished. All of these erasing inventions were hard to use and costly for any company in need of someone to type. Now in the year 2011, I am thinking as I write these pages on the Word Processor of my computer that the present way of typing is extraordinary, specially the fact that there is no erasing to be done, just elimination or errors quickly and effectively. I look down to my pages on the screen while I pleasantly enjoy the fruits of progress in the world of typing and duplicating documents on my magnificent PC. But, what I really wanted to say is that my Church community had had a retreat, a very important one since it is the weekend when the Catholic Church celebrates the feast of Pentecost which means Fifty days after Easter (or Passover) when the apostles while hiding from the Romans in the company of The Lord's mother and our mother The Virgin Mary, received the Holy Spirit according to the Scriptures. This is what Jesus Christ said to his disciples before He ascended into Heaven, that He has to go so that

He could send the Spirit to His Church to empower it and tend to its needs. My Church Community celebrated this special feast praying, singing and celebrating the Liturgies prepared for the Church for this important Day. The Holy Spirit passed through the Assembly and all of us (brothers and sisters) expressed in the most joyful way the presence of the Third Person of the Holy Trinity among us as promised by The Lord Himself. With this feast, Easter season is over and The Church would continue the Liturgy of the Hours of what it is called "Ordinary Time" until its next season which will be before Christmas. Blessed be The Lord who maintains The Church, His Bride until the end of times, giving us the opportunity to live by Grace and in Love.

My mother Elizabeth Lopez Salazar, a widow, was the daughter of an elegant civil service worker (one of the first eligible bachelors of Madrid who would wear a cape) making him very well-known at the different levels of society. My grandfather belonged to the generation of the year 1919 even though he was born during the end of the 18th century. My mother was the granddaughter of a rich jeweler who had a jewelry store and several properties in the best areas of the capital of Spain but despite their fortune, the family was hard working and involved with the popular street life. One of the first gas cars which was driven in the streets of Madrid belonged to my mother's grandfather and she was very proud of it and used to talk to us about this car all the time. All together a family with class and "cache" My mother as a single girl was a pretty blond with a beautiful smile, brown bright eyes and the skin of a Hollywood diva. She wasn't tall but had a perfect small framed figure and during the family's visits to the city of Cadiz, a small but busy harbor in the south of Spain, she attracted many suitors who one by one were rejected by my mom because she said that she wasn't ready for marriage life since she had plans to enter in the Opera Academy and learn how to sing opera. She had a beautiful voice and she would've been a great singer if God in His Infinite Wisdom would not have planned for my father to be and my mom to fall in love and get married before my mom's 20th birthday. In this family who lost their good fortune during the Spanish Civil War, God planted my roots and I was born with a few ill family genes and the desire to become republican as soon as I would be old enough to vote. Such political views were a heritage on my grandfather's side who was a Republican at heart and who passed to his daughter, my mother, a love for justice and freedom she carried all her life, but my mother was leaning towards the right wing and was faithful to Franco's regime until that, after his death, she starting to vote for the Socialist Party and there was nothing that anybody could do about it. I was proud of my family's political diversity and tried to abstain from entering into discussions with any of them. Unfortunately when I to become a woman, I put my cards on the table and started showing my preferences towards the left wing and sometimes I would have to defend my political views with as much passion as I could. Later on when I was brought back into the bosom of the mother Church, my choices became more towards the center of the political arena and I always tried to be on the side of the Church and struggle to build the Kingdom of Heaven on Earth. My mother was a Socialist until her death and she supported the party with her patriotic empathy. All together a family with a diverse personality, mentality and political views but on top of everything a great love and spirit of sacrifice where children were a priority and we were taught to put them first no matter what, a thought that made me wait and try to save my marriage all I could until my strength left me and my mind couldn't think straight anymore and I decided to start a new life and the pursuit of happiness. God was already working in saving this family and He let me go my way till His time would come.

I will continue with the story of my mother. She became some widow young (she was 37 years old) with 6 small children, no fortune, job, a house or a profession. In this difficult situation, my mother decided to sell all our goods and go back to Madrid, the town where she was born. And so we did. Once there we went to live at my grandmother's flat, an old building situated in the famous neighborhood called Salamanca in front of the beautiful and famous Retire Park where me and my brothers spent the evenings with our friends playing and talking. I've loved to take walks through the trees, observing the many fountains and statues of popular heroes and saints. Many times when coming back to Madrid by myself, I went back to the beautiful and familiar Retire and sometimes even walking through the same old trees, I will enjoy a Book's Fair went through all those interesting books and spent time there by my grandmother's flat remembering my time with her, with my young brothers and sisters and my mother who tried very hard to keep us together, made a living and nurse my grandmother and her sister Joy who was blind, retired and a very hard to please elderly woman. She was never married and the only family who cared for her was my beautiful grandmother who gave her life for her because once when we were at the table, my great aunt became disoriented and was walking towards a wall and my grandmother stood up from the table and starting to reach her before she'd hit herself against the wall. My grandmother had an ill knee and she couldn't move well but she was able to help her sister even though her leg resented the sudden move and she was housebound from that moment on. My brothers and sisters used to help nurse aunt Joy and I believe that such experience of taking care of an elderly lady, made us more concerned and able to serve at (from) a young age.

My uncle lived with us until he decided to get married and he was always a perfect host and company to us. My mom had a younger brother but he died when he was a child. His name was Michael and that is the reason why we named our younger son Michael John the names of both my uncles with the idea of keeping those names alive in the family. I don't remember very clearly how long were we at my grandmothers but I remember that Franco's Regime decided to build blocks of apartments for all the widows and poor families who qualified and so once more, we moved to the small apartment which would be our home until we started to go away and live our own lives. I was still there when I met my husband and we used to walk back and forth through the neighborhood visiting the Bars and greeting the neighbors who already knew that my boyfriend was an American and they approved of him because he spoke Spanish well and he was friendly and nice. When we moved my grandmother and uncle were sad even though they understood that we needed to have our own home but I used to visit them as often as possible and so did my mom. As soon as we got installed my mother started going out, more often that I liked and because my brother and sister were still very young, she would live them to my care, something that I did because I loved my family very much and I didn't want anything bad to happen to them but this task gave me too much responsibility and I was forced to matured in a hurry and made me bitter towards my mother because I had no social life. All that changed after I got my first job and started making my own money.

My mother Elizabeth Lopez died on the 22nd of December 2009. Soon will be two (2) years that she has passed over to the other side. Why do I say passed over and not gone because she is not gone, she is alive on Eternal Live mode? That summer precisely during the month of August, I went to Madrid to be with her…maybe to say farewell to her. The last time that I saw her, she didn't look so well and I saw in her eyes shadows instead of light. It is difficult to explain considering that after all it is my mom I'm mentioning in this page and I missed her terribly and even though we did not always enjoy a perfect relationship I think that as mother and daughter we communicated well. While I was at her apartment situated in a nice area of Torreon de Ardor, I tried to accompany her as much as possible and I also tried not to argue since somehow I knew that she would die soon. When I left to come back home to the States, I explained the best that I could, about death and the possibility of one of us dying soon taking on the fact that I was flying and that there is always a risk. I talked about God, Eternal Life, Heaven, Hell, going to another life.... joining her relatives, etc. I remember well that I explained this delicate subject in a way which I've considered clear and tender at the same time. It wasn't easy and I give the Glory to God once more because I knew that those words have been inspired by the Holy Spirit. I came back home at the end of August, maybe at the beginning of September and I went to Massachusetts to visit my sister and brother in law who are also doing missionary work in that State. As soon as I saw them I told them that mom was dying and not to wait too long to see her and reconciled with her as I have done and that would be the best that we could do for her and of course also pray for a peaceful passing and the salvation of her soul. They were going to Spain during the month of December and already had their plane tickets for December 17th. On the 20th I received an email informing me that mom was seriously ill and that she has been taken to the hospital. I had plans to spend Christmas with my son the priest and on the 22nd took the train to Maryland. I remember that just getting to the parish, both my son and I heard the news that my mom has passed away. One of my nephews communicated to my son's cell and my son told me. We hugged and held each other for a few minutes and decided at that moment that we will not travel to Spain because of the time difference we would be late for her passing. I didn't want to go to the cemetery and missed her funeral all together; for me it would it been too cold and distant and I decided to stay with my son instead and pray for her during the following days which we did and it was beautiful for us to remember her in all the Masses and mourn her in Church and with the Church. I felt that I had made peace with her before I left and that fact filled my soul with consolation and tenderness beyond my expectations and again I knew deep inside that God's plan had been done.

To see some members of my family destroyed makes me angry and sad, both feelings are negative and difficult to handle and it makes me suffer every time I think of them. The family was in trouble before we encountered Conversion, God showed Himself to us and called us to His Church and God was faithful and merciful because He called first the ones most in need. My younger brother was married to an alcoholic woman who used to spend more time in a nearby Bar than at home or with her children. She was a very violent nature because during her teenage years she rebel against her parents and left home a couple of times until she had to be locked up in a Juvenile Institution when her parents found out that she has been pregnant by my brother and the way for her to go free was for my brother to marriage her and, even though she was under aged, her parents gave her permission to marry. I guess she'd probably felt that she was forced to get married even though she was very much in love with my brother and crazy about him but because of the circumstances, she always felt that her life couldn't have been different if she wouldn't have gotten pregnant. The truth of the matter was that they weren't ready to live together as my brother had to stop his education and get a job to maintain her. He tried to get a good job but he wasn't ready so he wasn't making much money and problems started very soon in their marriage. My sister in law was used to stay in bed till late in the afternoon, didn't like to clean or cook and she was barely making it in her house chores and my brother was used to be home and be served, didn't have a lot of experience with woman and after he lost a couple of jobs, decided to stay home in bed with her pregnant wife. The solution to their lack of financial support was to start getting friends in need of a place to live as long as they'd support them. This arrangement was acceptable in the beginning and things were working to my brother's delight until problems started to interfere with the happiness of the young couple. My sister in law continued drinking during her pregnancy and as a consequence of it, the baby was born prematurely; it was a beautiful baby girl and she made it by the grace of God who was starting to make a story of Salvation for the family. The baby stayed in the hospital in Intensive Care for almost three months and the immediate family would visit and everybody believed that everything was alright. But it wasn't and my mother started to see all the mistakes that they were making. Things deteriorated little by little and my brother and his alcoholic and bitter wife started to have the fights which would accompany them until my brother started going to Church, found a New Life in Jesus and change was beginning to make everybody uneasy.

Continuing with my family's history I've also experienced my life after my first job which was arranged by my mother's older brother John which is also my younger son's second name given to him in memory of both of my mom's brothers as I've already explained earlier in this book. I should say "this book" because I might just as well write another, we'll see. I was also saying about how I felt when left alone babysitting day in and day out when all I wanted was to go out and have fun with my friends; I don't even know how I had the friends but I did manage to enjoy a few good friends during my teen years and that made my life more bearable, even though I was allowed to go out on Sundays. But somehow The Lord made it possible for me and my sisters to have some fun during our growing years and now I see it that way. I used to play with my baby sister and made believe that my middle finger and my finger were the legs of a (emanate) and the game consisted of talking to my sister through the little guy and asking her questions about school and how her day went. The results were excellent and we talked for hours and both had a lot of fun. This game lasted for years and it made our relationship better and very open. It happened that many years later, we would remember those moments and had a complicity between us that we didn't have with the other sisters and I realized that it had created a deep awakening and trust, which I believed was very necessary during my mother's long absences. My strong feeling of guilt brought about many arguments between my mother and I since every time that she would try to communicate with me about anything, I would react like I was being accused and explode causing my mother to get frustrated and angry at me, the feeling of rejection took over and the relationship suffered because it was cut even before it would have started. I am very glad that the year that my mother passed away, I went to visit her and spent the month of August with her trying to be a "good" daughter and be at peace with her because somehow I knew that she wasn't going to live long. The experience was positive and we had some good moments but the best was while talking to her as my day to leave came closer, I've told her that we've better say goodbye and reconciled because this

Summer could be our last one together. At first, she didn't want to accept but God inspired me with the necessary words and my mom agreed to accept my petition for forgiveness and she also asked me to forgive her which made the trip worth it and meaningful. The whole encounter gave me peace of mind and I left Spain feeling consoled and saying goodbye to my mom inside. I started praying for her from that moment on and asked my sons and the rest of the family to also pray for her passing. I believe that prayer helped her to die the peaceful death that she had. According to my sister who is also doing Missionary work in the USA she had fallen into a semi- coma right after she visited her at the hospital and she never woke up. Blessed is The Lord and full of Mercy because He took my mother in a very gentle way and her death brought over reconciliation with the whole family particularly with the sister who provided a beautiful Church funeral for her where she received the sacraments which are the help that a Christian soul needs to pass to the other world and continued her way to Heaven.

In Spain while I lived there alone and divorced, I was always looking for work and money. I needed money to pay for my son's school (now public education is free) for food, clothing, public transportation and of course for drinks and socializing. Sometimes I think back and feel remorse because I would like to have been a better mother, responsible, and always there for my children; loving and willing as a "normal" mother would be but I wasn't like that. I was sick and without values. My moral teachings had left my soul, my spiritual upbringing disappeared as if by magic and my heart was empty and rotten, unable to care for anybody that wasn't myself. I know that my children suffered because I wasn't there for them and because I've left their father. The whole family was dysfunctional, crazy and careless, living a false dream, a life without order nor structures and the necessary presence at home. Divorce is evil, out of order. It makes the relationships worse than before. It makes the children close themselves into shadows and their instincts get out of control endangering their lives and the natural growth process. I cannot change the past, I can only turn it into a better future and that is what I did with the help of God and the support and guidance of the Church. The suffering is still there though The Lord has made us happy beyond our wildest dreams and now my sons and I enjoy a mature relationship. I still don't understand what got into me and the only explanation would be that the influence of evil gets into you more and more. The same way that good goes around and turns bad deeds into good, so does evil and becomes worse because one wrong decision creates another and every action brings consequences which we cannot see because we cannot see into the future as God does and that is how He can make a different future for any wrong present. Eternity is never ending and in that type of time everything can be changed for better or worse. I don't know if I'm making myself clear even though I'm trying very hard to explain my thoughts. There is a big battle going on and it will last until the New Era starts. Jesus talks about another coming, the first coming when He was born into a man from The Virgin Mary, the second is an individual and personal coming and the third is what The Bible calls the "Parousia", the end of the world as we know it, the Judgment and the beginning of His Kingship in the New Kingdom, the Kingdom Which He was announcing and that He told to Pilate who was the Governor of Galilee during His trial and crucifixion. My life and the life of my family was one of the reasons why Jesus had to die because He paid a price for me, my husband and my sons and for every member of the family who had seen this. Without this necessary intervention I would still be in my sins and blind to real life. The condition of men is this reality as we are all born in sin the "Original Sin" I don't know if this can be understood. Now we (Humanity) may go farther from the truth and from God or become closer if we listen to the Message of Salvation and receive the forgiveness of our sins. But without a Church who announces this story, we will not be saved from ourselves and from evil.

Fresno, 11/13/2015- I am what is referred to as a "Baby Boomer" which is someone born during the demographic birth between 1946 and 1964. I really made it by a lucky chance as I was born during the first month of 1946. These 're the years according to the United States Census Bureau, as Landon Jones, who coined the term "baby boomer" in his book Great Expectations: America and the Baby Boom Generation, defined the span of that generation as extending from 1943 through 1960, and authors William Strauss and Neil Howe, define the social generation of Boomers as the cohorts born from 1943 to 1960 who were too young to have any memory of World War II, but old enough to remember the postwar American High. The Golden Boomers are retired or will retire soon from any social-cultural occupation or profession. In my case I agreed, as I retired from working in the Public Schools a few years ago and I've always had jobs of great responsibility towards social as well as economic issues. I have no memory of war except the Vietnam one and that's because my deceased husband Carl asked to be assigned to that country and in His infinite wisdom, The Lord sent him to Spain to meet me. Culturally oriented Boomers are everywhere. Some very famous ones are the Beatles, Rolling Stones produced in The United Kingdom, writers like Allen Ginsberg, etc. I have been connected with music as well as literature mostly from Spanish writers. One famous singer and author of most of his songs is Joan Manuel Serrate, the well-known passionate Catalan, and many others. Joseph Albireo is a Baby Boomer and is now "Doctor Honoris Causa" by different Colleges and Universities. His last book "Kerygma" has changed the lives of thousands of people who had forgotten what life is all about.

As a group, they were the healthiest and wealthiest generation to that time and amongst the first to grow up expecting the world to improve with time and did everything within their power to take part in the progress of Europe and America. Schools of all kinds, Universities and local Colleges, were full of willing participating young adults who became doctors, pilots, engineers of every type, health professionals and many inventions were created during those years as well as investigations towards science and the military. Baby Boomers were good workers and rebuilt little by little what has been destroyed and forgotten.

Many movements started and were started by them, business and factories that provided jobs that opened doors for the future.

Philadelphia, PA 08/13/2015

After my husband and I divorce (late 80's, We've been separated for 3 years before he (Carl) decided to send me the divorce paper through his lawyer, my life was a total mess. The boys were depressed, even though they lived with family, went to a good school and were well and cared for. They were separated from each other as I lived at my younger brother's place with my younger son, Michael-John and Chris, the older, lived with my mom who wanted him to keep her company. I was trying really hard to visit him during weekends and holidays but the truth is that I had my mind on other things, pressed by many problems, different relationships and looking for work to help the family. In those days, sometimes I would think that we lived in a "commune" (a way of life from the hippy era were people, mostly couples) would join with homeless from either sex, sometimes people who had been in jail and didn't have a place to live. This unusual way of life, reminds me of Joseph Albireo and Joy Fernandez, both new for the far away from the Church and also for those like me and some of the members of my family who, though baptized, were not practicing Catholics. I should explain Catechumenate: a name given to the type of instruction given to the candidates for baptism which lasted a precise length of time, after which, they would be ready to be baptized. For those already baptized, but fully instructed, is the neo (or again) re-discover

We talk about Joseph and Joy who together as a team with Father Mario, an Italian priest started the first Christian community at the Shantytowns of Madrid and Rome, among the more poor and rejected from society, even outlaws.

Fresno, CA: May 11 - about the conversion of my younger sister Angela.

Angela received the gift of faith in Spain, on the beach and at the precise moment when she was trying to take her life and draw. It's all very dramatic but true and when a person is desperate, God can intervene if given the chance. I am sure we have some people praying and interceding for the family in Heaven or Purgatory and that is probably the reason why so many of its members have been helped when in need. May God continue working with the History and in the History of this family and many other families who are so in trouble and in need of His intervention and Mercy.

Angela and her husband, Valero became missionaries later on and were sent to the USA, to help a parish and also to evangelize[1*]

Today Wednesday 7 of March 2012, I've been watching a couple of programs which are popular because I wanted to see what made them popular and why? One is "American Idol", the other," America's next model" and I try to watch them with an open mind to no avail. The "idols to be" are too eager to make it but no willing to give all that they have. This is my personal critical opinion and I am entitled because I am an adult who watches TV and I have the right to observe and use my observations to the best of my knowledge and so I do. I try to keep an open mind while sitting on the sofa in my living room to no avail as my mind was thinking that those programs are about dreams almost impossible to reach and far from the real American Way of Life, which is very much unique and reachable until our present days. A way created out of a desire for freedom of Religion, same rights for everyone, respect and "love of neighbor" and all this done "under God" and with His Blessings. Hard work never killed anyone and to pay just taxes was a duty and the proper way to have a supply of honest earned money which was used for the good of all and the safety of the country. Unfortunately, those "rights" are not clear, explained nor respected anymore and our "way of Life" is very much in danger of losing its efficacy and its power. "Freedom of Speech" has been changed by "politically correct", the "common good" has been transformed into "I come first and the hell with everyone else".

Because of the trauma caused by the unacceptable death of my father, I looked for his affection in men which led me to fornication and later, adultery. My relations with the opposite sex were very dysfunctional because, in my mind, I was to receive all the attention and affection that I didn't get as a child but wouldn't give any back. As a result of such behavior, I would look for different relationships, use them and leave them to seek a new love and so on…

I was in a bad situation but I didn't know it and continued on this search for my father's love. Several years passed in this sick quest since all my relations with men will leave me empty and frustrated which will take me back to nightclubs, drinking and looking for more. My mother tried to ignore this situation and just acted as if nothing was wrong though she would constantly put me down, criticize all my choices, use me as a free babysitter and made my life a difficult one. She will constantly compare me to my father, complaining about his alcoholic behavior and abuse. Our relationship was unhealthy and many times we would argue bitterly even though I would usually be the one crying and running away to my room. Only after I went back to church and heard that God is my Father, this dependence ended. I learnt to be a people's pleaser very early in life, always looking for my own satisfaction and interests., but my mother was impossible to please. Though I have had many boyfriends, I was still a virgin at the age of 23 more for fear of losing the sign of my good uprising than by choice, so when my sister came back from England and told me that she wasn't a virgin anymore, I was determined to stop being one. I remember my mother taking me out of school at an early age but I don't remember why, though the reason seemed to be my lack of interest in studying and getting good grades. Sometimes I think that it was because she needed me to get a job and help with the expenses but I am not absolutely sure. Later on in life, I felt very proud of being the only daughter who helped my mother and my younger siblings because it made me feel really good and responsible. It is true that only when man finds His Creator man becomes an adult and though he is still the creature but he/she reaches maturity and understanding as written in The Bible. It is a natural law of and I see, when I look around me, that Humanity is turning for the worse because it is made of uneducated and immature people without a purpose in Life, constantly looking for happiness and never satisfied. I was like that, like a ship without a pilot, like a sheep without a shepherd, all alone in the immensity of the Universe. A person can become crazy in that situation. I almost did.

You know you are getting old when you put lipstick on without looking into a mirror…(Maria Agnes Martin) "yourself in the mirror"

Because my husband was also an alcoholic, after our reconciliation and because we didn't have the support of a Christian Community until the year 1990, I joined one of the support groups for the families of the alcoholic called Alanson and I received a lot of tools and was educated on the illness. I know that in an alcoholic family each member covers one another and everybody plays a role which is assigned by the illness and puts each other against one another. Reality becomes something that cannot be touched because the alcoholic person is supposed to be protected and blinded so that he/she would not see and therefore not to know. I remember the commercial which compared the illness with an elephant walking in the living room which nobody sees or chooses not to see and everybody goes about their business as usual. I know that I've had been exposed to the illness but it wasn't for long and though the "seed" has been planted in the deepest of my being, it didn't cause too much damaged so that I was able to keep some of the values my mother implanted in us, helping to form some kind of a conscience. Also the fact that we had received a Catholic education meant a difference when making our personal choices in life. For example, both my older brother and sister marry in Church and started a regular "normal" life but of course in a secularized world as this, "normal" has lost its meaning and decisions have no real value, so most of us do what we have been manipulated to do but don't know it. The Catholic church has been accused of being too radical which is the right way to be because it is by being "one-sided" that we can see things in the right perspective. Good if good, bad if bad, black or white, right or wrong etc. these are concepts which must come back to our daily vocabulary and because being radical means from or to the root, it is a very safe place to be (in the root) or close to the root to be able to see better how things grow from the beginning and how are they growing so that whatever doesn't come from the same root, would be eradicated (pull off) when the time is right (Jesus said to His disciples to let things grow together until it will be time to intervene) and that is a just rule I think. I take sides every day and I need to do so because, as a member of the Church, I am a light or part of the light which would illuminate a dark spot somewhere or sometime and I also have a mission which is to announce the risen Lord with my own life, my attitudes, actions and decisions, stepping on the ladder towards Heaven showing the way to all the souls which might come after me or behind me. This is my life (or details of it) before Christ and after Christ (B.C. & A.D.)

But he (my father) was a good provider and a loving father. He was with my mother until his death. My mother told us that the night he died, they were both in bed and my father was out of breath and tried to sit when all of a sudden he fell back on his side of the bed in slow motion and died after a short while. My mother was by his side and held him for a few minutes, then she called my cousin the nurse, who came over immediately and helped with the arrangements and preparations necessary. I remember the body being placed in his coffin in the middle of the living room with candles on the corners and people weeping dressed in dark clothes. Because nobody talked to me about him being dead or passing or anything in reference to his death, I was in a dip crisis for many years until I was reached by the Church and its announcement of Salvation and understood the death of my father and accepted it in the Lord. Also, thanks to the Church I understood that alcoholism is the "secret illness" and that in an alcoholic family each member covers one another and everybody plays a role assigned to protect the alcoholic and to put every member of the family against each other. Reality becomes something that cannot be touched because the alcoholic is kept blind and away from it so that he/she can continue drinking thinking that everything is alright and that drinking is a social act which doesn't hurt anybody. I remember the commercial about an elephant being in the middle of the family room and everybody going about their daily business as usual. I know that I've been exposed to the sickness but not for long and even though the seed was planted in the deepest of my being, didn't caused too much damage because of the values that my mother implanted also in us which helped to form some kind of a conscience and of course the Catholic education which we received influenced our family to make the proper choices in life. For example, both my older brother and sister married in the Church and started a more or less regular life but in a secularized world like this, those values have lost their meaning and most of us are being manipulated into doing what we want regardless of its moral value. The Catholic church has been accused of being too radical but that is the right way to be since, only by being "one-sided" things can be seen in the right perspective. Good or bad, black or white, write or wrong, etc. are concepts which need to come back to our vocabulary. Radical comes from the word "root" and it means to be safe (deep in the root of things) to be able to see better the growth of something that is beginning to grow and therefore, whatever is not growing the right way could be "eradicated" (pull off) before it starts causing future damage. Yes, I must take sides sometimes, almost every day and I need to do it because, as a member of the Church, I am a light or part of one which illuminates any dark spot which could make us stumble and fall. The Church has a Mission and I have a Mission: to announce the risen Lord to the world with my own life, my attitudes, my choices, actions and decisions. I must step on the ladder towards Heaven showing the way to all the souls which happen to follow behind me. This is my life (or details of it) before Christ and after Christ (B.C & A.D.)

Philly PA About Baptism 08/26/2015 Part of the catechesis by Pope Paul VI St. Augustine says: "If we cannot have the Catechumenate beforehand, we'll carry it out afterwards, that is, the instruction, completion and education, the whole of the Church's educative work. The sacrament of Christian regeneration must once again return to being what it was in the consciousness of the first generation of Christians on the first norms of the Church. One of the things that has happened is that the preparation has been liturgically concentrated in the baptismal rite. The liturgy in fact still bears traces of this preparatory initiation which preceded baptism, and which during the early times when society was profoundly pagan, was called the catechumenate. Later the Church condensed the period because all families were Catholic, all were "good" Christians. Now this complete education, instruction needs to be done after baptism, into the proper lifestyle of Christians. I am finally connected to the one I needed to be connected to, Jesus Christ the Son of God, head of the Church, as long as I'm a member of the same body (the Church) (St. Augustine bishop's sermon 33-week ordinary time second: "The Lord is at hand; have no anxiety." That is the reason why everyday life's activities, cultural oriented events, the Media at all levels (film making, fashion shows, news disclosure, advertisement-advertising, every kind of design for commercial reasons has taken a turn for the worse because is no longer based on the rich Judeo-Christian tradition roots and has lost the sense of what is real, what is true. By going back in the right direction, society might have a chance to have a better, peaceful quality of life and the future that God promises for us if we follow His way.

According to the reading from the treatise on Forgiveness by St. Fulgent of Ruse bishop. (33 weeks in ordinary time –Liturgy of the hours- to reach this total change into the perfection needed to enter into Heaven (Purgatory is created for this purpose) men shall be transformed from a shameful state to a glorious one. St John the evangelist says: "We are now the sons of God; what we shall be has not the jet being revealed, but we know that when it is revealed we shall be like him, because we shall see him as he is. (When this prophecy is fulfilled, then it will be the sight.)

Today is Friday the 17th of August 2012 and I'm going to write the second draft of the story of My Life, a story of some of my life because I don't remember all of it and I think that it is a very long one. I am now 66 years old and I feel that I'm old enough to write my story or, at least, the part that is more important, more real and to talk about the things that made it what it is now, the decisions that I've made in the past direct me towards my present. So I think that I should start: My name is Maria Agnes Gonzales Martin even though my "American name" is only Agnes Martin and "the Martin" belongs to my husband whose ancestors came from Cordoba, Spain and that last name is very popular in that country which is where I was born. This summer my son Michael (the priest) and I spent two wonderful weeks there and Antonio, the responsible of one of the Christian Communities in the Andalusia's region told us that fact about my husband's family name. Let's continue with the personal details of My Life: I was born to a couple who married for love, in the isle of Gran Canary in the capital Las Palmas. I am the third of 6 children, second daughter and, because I was born feet first (backwards in the womb), my birth was considered a "lucky one". I've already said that I am 66 so you know that the year of my birth was 1946 and that was a "very good year." I would say something about that particular year and "Baby Boomers" later in the book. I shall continue…My mother was from Madrid so that made her a "madrilène" and let me explain that when I started to write my mother was 88 years old and still with us, she passed over during the year 2009 a few days before Christmas day and that is why I've said that my mother "was" from Madrid. She was born in the year 1922 and the only daughter of a republican also from Madrid and my grandfather who was one of the first men to wear the popular and elegant Spanish style cape and also had a car from the Ford Company. He was a politician and a romantic and my grandmother was very much in love with him and my mother was the apple of his eye and very proud of him. My lovely grandparents had also a son, John and he is in another section of the book because he was a very important person for me and my siblings. My mother had another brother and his name was Michael who only lived a few years and my son, the priest, wears both my mother's brothers name. So my son's name is Michael John. The uncle who died while a child became our "mysterious uncle" and because children are very generous and give their love to all relatives, alive or dead, we gave both our uncles a place in our hearts. My father was a local, an islander, a strong built fellow of dark complexion and a beautiful smile. He fell in love with my mother at first sight and, after a short courting time, got married. My mother, a hard hearted woman, told us that if my father would've lived longer, they would've had 6 more children and that was that. When my father died in 1956, I was 10 years old and I don't remember much about it, but I kept some memories of him and most are good. He was a family man and proud of all his children, sad to say that he was particularly proud of my brothers but even I can understand that. He used to celebrate all our birthdays and invite relatives and friends over and he used to drink. My mother said that he was an alcoholic and she was probably right though I've never seen him out of control and don't remember any scandal or big fights or even verbal abuse so, either I am in denial or he wasn't a violent man. Anyway alcoholism is the "secret illness" so even if he was, we wouldn't know much about it. I remember our first communion ceremonies and he was always there, though I don't remember him to take us to Mass on Sundays or ever praying at the dinner table

We all possess a gift given to us by God, our free will and it is something so extraordinary and divine that by itself would prove the existence of a Creator with a higher Intelligence and that us being here is not a coincidence or a product of the "big bang" theory and anyhow, this fact means that we cannot be obliged nor forced to do anything against our own will. If you think about it, it's a magnificent power and given only because we had been created with great love, care and purpose and if we don't see this, it is because we don't have the knowledge of the existence of God in our lives. The Church knows this and helps science by cooperating in every possible way and means. It is so that we get in trouble only when we make the wrong choice or choices and we become victims of abuse or crime if we let it happen to us. Good or bad actions come predetermined by our own decisions and nothing that we want bad enough would be denied to us because our will power can work wonders in any situation. To ignore this would be to lose a great deal of actions resulting in future cases or new problems without the solution which comes from knowing the root of these (the problems) This gift, as I was saying, we use it to accept what we see as good or convenient and, best of all, we use it to look for the will of God for us at that moment in history and to live it in our story, the story God is doing or creating with us and for us and, once we accept His will for us then we go ahead and fulfill it. It is done! And so, as we see, our free will is a very powerful and necessary tool for any person who needs to make the right decision every chance we have. Anyway, I was talking about these popular programs "American Idol" and America's Next Model" that I was watching the 7th of March on TV, and I couldn't help to feel sorry for all those young people who want to be famous and popular and maybe even rich and happy pursuing these so called "fashion dreams". Let me explain why I was feeling sorry and what that has to do with our great gift of "free will": were they doing what they wanted? I do not Think so and why do I think that? Because they were following the instructions given by two may be managers and one of them also a photographer who was taking shots while the models changed positions and facial expressions constantly. These women from their early 20's to early 30's were just there, dressed as extremely as possible, their hair tinted of different colors and combed in sophisticated styles, their make-up heavy and plastic- like. The theme of the session was mother and daughters, baby food, formula bottles, baby spoons, etc. What did they have to do? Act and look like babies, try to get baby expressions on their faces and bodies, all the time trying to grab and touch "mommy" and get her attention and care. The managers kept giving them instructions and scolding them if they did anything not to his liking. The models looked bored or even worse resigned and the whole affair looked pathetic to me but of course, I am old and my mentality is different and more according to my age than to theirs. My point is that I didn't see these young beautiful women using their free will even once and they were all for the session to please the instructors and to win their approval certainly! When I left my husband taking our sons away from him, I was convinced that I was using my free will and I was sure that I was doing what I wanted: to run away from unhappiness and abuse and to pursue the real happiness I had the right to have but how wrong I was! Yes, I wanted to be happy then and I want to be happy now but I wasn't using my free will as a gift from God but as a negative and evil power which took me on the road towards destruction and despair as I could experience later on when I was trying to find love in all the wrong places and I really lost myself in the winding spiral of all my wrong choices. When I finally sat on one of the old benches in the Church to listen to the Good News, I was so destroyed that I couldn't even talk. It took a while for me to start making any sense and not after I begin to use the language (the new language) of the spirit, I could have made myself understood by the other people in the Christian small community that God had created to begin in us the work that He had to do to bring us all back to reality and to being well again. Now after all these years in Church, I can still remember how awkward I felt when I discovered that I had been deprived of my human dignity and all my rights had been removed by my own lack of self-sufficiency and pride. God little by little gave me back my right to make decisions, my dignity and self control and by the time we went back home, I was already beginning to feel the healing power of having my own will power return to me. Society is going the wrong way and it is not too late to return (turn back) to the right one which is like it has always been, the way to goodness and righteousness, and even though we are still using the words of our ancestors, we are not using their knowledge nor their acceptance of God. "In God we trust" the beautiful and sincere motto that appeared (for now) on our money, was not just a propaganda affirmation (as our enemies had said) but the result of a well sturdy and well thought action of faith taken even to the money which was put "under God" as everything else was. So my point today was to explain what having free will means for us as free people and where does it come from to ask to be defended at all times and appreciated because it is something that we receive from our Creator to use it for our good and the good of those around us and beyond. God Bless America and it's Freedom, and the freedom that He gave me!.

At the Airport while waiting for the airport police officer to let us go, I begged like I've never had…There was an African-American sitting on a bench by the side of a small waiting area and he looked tired. The police officer pointed at him and said to me: "Look at that man! He has been waiting for three days and he is not going anywhere because nobody leaves without the right legal documents" and shouting: "nobody" and turning to me and my sons he said: "officer take this woman and her children to the US Embassy and then, turning back to me and with a perplex look on his face, he said to the same officer who was waiting in front of him: "no, take them to the plain. They are waiting". I almost cried out: "Thanks", and started walking towards the Gate. The people who were listening and waiting to see the development of such an unusual event, clapped happily and some of them accompanied us the rest of the way. My sons were laughing and I was in Heaven because I had seen the Red sea opening in front of my eyes, a stupendous miracle happening right there for us and for everyone who was ready to see it and believed. With a sense of thanksgiving in my heart, I hurried towards my future, my new life while deep inside I was giving thanks to God for His divine and wonderful intervention in this difficult affair while showing us and others His power and His love. The plane crew was waiting for us and, smiling, helped us to our seats making sure that our seat-belts were fastened and then the airplane started moving to take off and I thought: "take us home" and finally relaxed on my seat. I remember praying: "Please God give my husband time to get to know his sons and be a father to them until they grow up". When my husband passed away in 1995 both my sons were grown which showed that God accomplished His promises and answers prayers when these are said with a sincere heart. The flight was smooth and I was able to talk to my sons about their father which helped them to remember their relationship with him and made it easier for them to accept the new reality (which was) opening right in front of them and getting closer as the plane rushed through the sky leaving behind other reality, a false one because we've have failed to fulfill our life in the way which was intended by the will of God since marriage comes only from God and in Him only can be lived and that it's why marriage is in danger now that God in the person of the Son, Jesus Christ, has been taken out of it and even given to homosexuals corrupting the sacred order of love which, according to the law of Creation, was to be a sharing of a life with another where two persons become one and giving totally to each other enjoy Divine life together with the human one and making from the aridity of our hearts a well of abundant flowing love and since "Love is God" and "God is Love" it cannot performed it's total meaning when God is ignored during such enduring union. My marriage was meant to be and because of the Sacrament being valid it couldn't be destroyed. When I said yes to God's plan of reconciliation and the reconstruction of the broken pieces of my life, He immediately took over and, with my permission, put us back together again and showed to us the happiness which we had been looking for all of our lives.

The way that the announcement of salvation (the Good News/Gospel) is taken to the people feels to me with wonder. It is done in an amazing and soft go-around which only the Holy Spirit should be able to inspire. There is also some shaking as it happened to my younger sister Angela who was by the beach and while walking into the sea, suffered a transformation which changed her life. Most of the time it is an announcement and so clear to the ear that if it is God' will, you will hear it. I admire evangelizers who give their lives to save others, and go where they are sent without a doubt or a complaint. In the Neo-catechumenate, beginning right after the Vatican II Council during the years 1963-67, the Popes (Paul VI, John Paul II and the actual Benedict XVI) started to send families who were ready to go anywhere in the world. Many of them had 9, 12 or more children, mostly small babies and an "ad experimental" process started very much like the story of Exodus. Today, almost 50 years after, the implanting of the Domestic Church (Iglesias Domestic) continues where it is needed. One of those generous families is my sister's oldest son, his wife and their 8 children. They had been sent to Estonia to help the church there. They've been there for almost 5 years and the two younger children were born in that beautiful country by the Baltic sea. I didn't know then that my "yes" to be open to reconcile with my husband, would open a door to all these wonderful changes in my family who were so far away from the Lord and from His Church. So while searching for the truth, some of the members of this family had found the center, the core of life and we are happy. St. Paul says: "With sufferings, with tribulations, persecutions, hunger, loneliness…but nothing can separate us from the love of God. Many teams of catechists are preaching the gospel everywhere, sometimes constantly, and many people are coming back to Church, to join the body of Christ. Fresno in California where I've lived for almost 35 years, is a hard town to break the news to and it is not that the people there are not looking but their busy lives separated them from the truth. The economic crisis had hit almost every corner of the world and, according to some finance experts, "greed" had a lot to do with it. You shall not steal! It is one of the commandments and we do not understand that they were given to us for our protection. The Church uses its riches to help the poor and it has been so since it was founded by the Lord. We should all know that many charitable organizations had been ruled by the same principle: to provide aid for the needy, the poor, the hungry, etc. It is not that the Church keeps treasures (even though it has many), but the Church administers and cares for all its properties to serve us, Christians and non-Christians. When I came back home after my husband and I reconciled and by listening to the catequesis, I learnt the truth about the Church and accepted it. I opened my home to anyone who would be sent by the Church in need of hospitality. My husband, my sons and I were one of the first teams of catequists formed to announce the Good News or the News of Salvation in our home parish, St John's Cathedral. We did this for years and, when my husband passed away, my sons and I continued to do it until I was sent away to the Mission and my younger son went to one of the seminaries in the U.S.A. to be prepared to be a priest. Now when I go back home and I see all the new brothers and sisters who are walking in the Cathedral and other parishes in the diocese, I am grateful. I see the hunger for the word of God in California and everywhere and I pray to The Lord to send more workers to these fields. There is another vocation to the priesthood from the small communities of The Way. His name is Antonio and he is the second of 5-6 siblings and left for a seminary in India. When I see how happy he is I give glory to God who keeps providing for the spreading of the Kingdom and preparing the world for His second coming. I know that faith can only be given by the Holy Spirit but I also know that God in His infinite mercy wouldn't abandon us in the hour of need.

Fresno, May 2011

Before I was announced the Good News to I thought I had a good life. I've always made sure that I had a job, worked hard at it, tried to enjoy myself as much as I could, get along with my co-workers, please my mother and try to love her and not get angry at her. My daily life was about being myself, conned boys and used them to build my ego as much as possible, be a "nice girl" and take care of my siblings at home while I would live a double life since outside my home I was different and I even changed my name from Agnes to Lola to Marilo which sounded like a more sophisticated one. I didn't know then the harm that I was causing to my personality and how my mind was being transported into another reality which wasn't my own. I try to be extroverted but am very shy inside. I was quiet and had problems expressing myself and, while acting like a pro, I would remain silent and confused. With my boyfriends I would be a flirt, always reacting to their decisions and seeking their approval constantly while feeling rejected if they disagreed with me. I was a mess even though I thought that I was hot and more beautiful than my sisters or my friends and I know now that only the hand of God over me kept me from making bigger mistakes and/or being badly hurt as a teen. At school I didn't have many friends and later on when we moved to Madrid and mom placed both my younger sister and I in a charitable Institution run by catholic nuns, I didn't make friends easily either. I would get in trouble for different reasons and had a few encounters with some of my classmates and it was because of these and other incidents that the nuns kept me under their protection and care most of the time. I remember that I used to love the attention and at the same time resented them for having such a close look into my life. Because of the difficult situation of my home life, I grew up with several personality complexes. Expressing my thoughts and feelings was very hard and I would observe life instead of living it through a window. The more I became frustrated, the more rebellious I would be and like St. Paul says: "I want to do good but it is evil that results on my actions and I do more harm than good" That is precisely the situation of man and that was my situation but I didn't know it then. Marriage wasn't any easier and it was clear that I didn't know what to do most of the time and even as a mother I was neurotic and very possessive of my children. I know now that I did the best I could and I would give them as much love and attention as I was able to. It is for all the mistakes of my life, the anger and the sufferings, the hurt that I caused to others and all the hatred that Jesus Christ gave His life for and this is the reason why I was saved by Him and why He became my Savior. That confused, resented and bitter woman was me, and, not that I looked back but when I do, I do not recognize the person writing these pages now. I hoped the story of my life would be a book one day, and perhaps help others who might be going through a similar situation. God is more powerful than any power, any suffering, any illness and any tribulation. He is the answer to the eternal question: "What am I doing here?" and "What is the meaning of life?". He is the goal of all our search, the subject of our affections, the Light which lightens our darkest moments, the Source of Life, the Consolation for all our tears and, as we get to know Him and accept Him, our path would become clearer and, on His own words: "our burdens light"

Union City N.J. Fresno, May 2011

This morning, I started walking through the neighborhood and liked it. My new life and my status as a missionary widow makes me introduce myself to the people near me. After a walk in the warm, nice sun, I entered a Nicaraguan restaurant greeted the owner, a woman who was sitting on a side table with two children, a boy and a girl her grandchildren as she told me later on. I decided to order a hearty soup made of beef, "Yuca" potatoes and carrots. The soup was served accompanied of white, tender rice which was delicious. I ate with "gusto" and content because the weather was in the low 50's and I needed to get warm, inside and out. The owner's daughter was waiting tables while the mother rested with her children. It was like being at home with this family and I felt good eating with them talking near me. Just before I finished eating, a man, also a relative, entered and sat by the owner and started talking to the children. One of the women made a comment to me about the little girl and immediately the man, the children's uncle, directed this question to me: "Where are you from" in Spanish of course and I said that I was from Spain. He repeated my answer to himself in a low voice while assenting with his head like if agreeing into his own thoughts. I continued making positive comments about the children and he stood up, said goodbye and left the restaurant. After the man left, the daughter asked me if I've come to the restaurant before and I told her that it was the first time and that I've just moved nearby and wanted to try the Central-American food. I've also told them that I was a missionary and that there is a family also from Spain who just came to live by the place. One of the women acknowledges the family with a nod and asked me what was a "missionary"? I was delighted by the question and started to explain the meaning of the word and also what it implies. Both women and one of the children, the older, were listening attentively to my explanation and to my surprise, the daughter asked me what do you have to do to become a missionary and I told her that you need to be sent by the Church and follow the part of the Gospel that refers to that particular calling. "Leave what you have and come with me." I've told them that I had left a state that I liked, California, my house, family, ten grandchildren, a job, friends and a community of brothers and sisters to serve the Church in an unknown place among strangers but that I was happy in my new place and those strangers had become also my brothers and sisters and that I could see the Church as a mother that welcomes me and cares for me. The women were impressed but not surprised and especially the mother had some idea of what it meant to be a missionary and what the church does. She was agreeing with my comments and had a look of joy on her face. Before I left the place, they invited me to take a menu home and order any time. The encounter was positive and I think that I've just made friends next door. Maybe soon I would be able to share my life story and announce to them the Love of God. Anyhow, this experience has helped me to get ready for to-night's Eucharist and enter into Sunday, the day of rest or Day of The Lord.

Fresno, Ca. May 6, 2015

Once upon a time there was a grandma and a mom. Both of them had a smile on their faces and looked alike. The gra-ma was big and bright and the mom was little and nice. Both shared the same love for a son and the son was happy because felt loved by them. The son was handsome and tall and because he was happy and also nice, he prepared a big bed for the G-ma and shared his bed with the mom. Their children were also happy because the mom and the g-ma pray to God in Church and the children saw this as they lived in the same house, they went to school and ate their dinner and lived happily ever after.

(This story was dictated to the author by one of her granddaughter 5 year old Judith)

One day it will be my turn to go and it's all right, like the Beatles song says because now I've received the Message of Salvation and I have hope that Heaven exists and somehow I've felt Eternity even for a split second (of a second) and because of that I know that there is life after death, yes the big dilemma has been resolved for me and for many members of the small communities that are appearing in the Church everywhere. That thought being carried in my mind and in my soul, makes all the difference. Man is afraid of death ontologically suffers from the "fear of death" and that fear slave us to sin. To sin is to go against God and to make wrong choices, freely and with a full intention of the will to go against the Will of God. It is not to eat the famous apple as most of the people think anyhow sin has to do with that event in Paradise when Adam and Eve his companion, disobey the order not to eat from the tree of knowledge situated in a special place in the Garden of Eden and that "wrong choice of the will" (their will) started the downfall of Humanity as we know it. Is it a children's night story? Serpent and all....? Or is it the beginning of sin, whose father is The Devil, to spread as the bad seed throughout all the World? I think that the Holy Scriptures contained the truth and that is the way that happened, and to me makes sense and even I've been told that there are other versions of it (the Bible speaks of two) I go for the first one written on the Book of Genesis because God can have created anything He sets His powerful to (into) from any material He chooses, whenever He decides to do it and anywhere He pleases. So there that is the answer, simple, uncomplicated and to the point. He placed the perfect couple to live in the perfect place and forever. The fact that the couple decided to do their will to "become like Him?" made the difference and there are consequences to our mistakes and to the wrongs that we do, even if they are done unintentionally. The typical expression "sorry" may be good enough when we step on someone's toe, but to have to say it constantly and for the same mistakes, it's not good. When we confess our sins (and even in the Scriptures) when the adulterous woman was delivered by Jesus from being stoned to death, He looked at her and told her: "Go and sin no more" and that was more an order (done in a very tender way) than a request. I read somewhere that " Love means never having to say Sorry" and it is an intelligent thought. The "passing" of our sister Rosa Nelly has placed a fix word in my mind: One day I will be in a nice looking pastel color coffin and my soul will go in from of the trial Court of the afterlife and I'm not trying to scare anybody but it is what comes to my mind more often than before she went away and it helps because "it's the thought that counts" and if it keeps me from sinning and walking closer and closer to the place kept for me in Heaven, the better. I need all the help I can get and I pray to all those who have gone before me to intercede for me in front of The Father that I would join them when my turn comes.

SPEAKING OF MARRIAGE

Speaking of Marriage in general or better yet, marriage as an institution but not "Institute" as some enterprise funded by members of a very solvent Company but as instituted by someone who "invented" or made Marriage, God Himself. This is a quote from the letter sent by the American Bishops in regards to Congress passing the legislation on homosexual marriages: "We worry that both marriage and the family will be undermined by this tragic presumption of government in passing this legislation that attempts to redefine these cornerstones of civilization". Yes, somebody has to speak up and it happens to be the Catholic Church which prays for homosexual individuals, shows compassion to them, allow them in their services and as members as long as "they'd sin no more...." which is what Jesus told the sinner woman whom the town's men brought to His feet because they wanted to try Him and asked Him for His opinion on the matter. Of course the men knew that the law gave them the right to stone any woman who was got in the act of committing adultery and they wanted to make Him look bad in front of the whole town but Jesus knew what had happened and without saying a word started to write on the dry soil, the Bible doesn't tell us what He wrote but it tells us that the men started to let the stones fell from their hands and one by one let the scene and disappear in silence. This is a clear example of the difference between the law of men and the laws of the Kingdom of Heaven as Jesus calls His Kingdom when He mentioned it and who else would teach us this difference except God Himself in the person of the son Jesus Christ? Marriage is a sacrament, one of the seven that He instituted and gave to the Church for her to administer to its members and The Holy Spirit gives us grace every time we receive these Sacraments. Marriage was created in the garden of Eden when the first man Adam was put under a deep sleep and a woman was created from one of his ribs and the first man, the father of all humanity said when he saw this woman:" This is flesh of my flesh and blood of my blood" and he was right and that is how the union of a man and "his" woman started being formed. Marriage is the union, by love, between a man and a woman who had freely decided to share their life together and they're committed to be open to receive and accept all the children that God provides for them, no limits. It is a match made in Heaven and only Heaven would make it work and it is because we don't have that relationship with the Creator the sacrament of Marriage is in crisis today. I'm speaking out of my own experience since my marriage was destroyed and from the moment that I say Yes to returning to the house of the Father (see the parable of the prodigal son) my marriage was saved and God gave me back all my family because after my husband and I remarriage, we became closer than before with the rest of my family and all of us enjoyed good relations with my in-laws too. The Church establishes the Sacrament, blesses and witnesses the union, cares for it, advises the couple when they're troubled, nurses their spiritual needs, welcomes and baptizes the children, educates them, visits them when they're sick and buries them when they die. Marriage is an all life commitment which introduces the family to the life of Grace and Love which comes from the Baptismal font and the waters of Life. Because of this, it cannot be commercialized or manipulated or used for tax purposes or made into something which it's not.

How did I plan to run away from my husband, my in-laws, my friends, my neighbors and the authorities of this country? Only God knows. What I know is that I planned it for a whole year and with a cold mind. A mind that, after I was awakened by the Holy Spirit through the preaching of the Gospel or Good News, I felt terrified of such cold blooded planning and how I had kept hidden all the details, how I looked for a job so that I would be able to save for the expenses of the trip and kept a separated account. How I even found a friend who would accompany me and help me with the children and with the luggage. Because this happened before my "conversion", I used to think that success comes after a good decision, thinking over the ' 'pros' ' and the "cons" carefully. The thought that took me to make the decision of living with my husband was: If I was to die this day, where would I like to be and what life would I be living? It is a very deep thought and I was convinced that I was doing the right thing because the answer would always be that I wanted to be happy. My motives were good, the action that I have taken was the wrong one. During the year I was to run away with my sons, I made arrangements to have my son's names and information on my Spanish passport and because they were young children I didn't need my husband's permission to get them out of the country. To make sure that I would have enough money for the trip and to live on until I would get a job, I worked for almost a year. I don't remember exactly how I purchased our plane tickets but I bought them and I had them hidden in a secret place. I would treat my husband normally and I made sure that he wouldn't notice anything different in our relationship and of course I wouldn't say anything to the kids in case they would tell somebody else and ruin the "perfect plan". A few weeks before the day of departure I called my older sister Elizabeth who used to live near London and she was shocked but happy that I wanted to be myself and live my life and also that I was going to see her and stay with her and her family for some time. She didn't try to convince me to stay and later on, after she divorced my brother in law, I began to believe that I have been the cause for her marriage falling apart but I didn't care about her problems since I had problems of my own. Years later I understood that her marriage had been in trouble for a long time but she just didn't have the heart to accept and act upon it like I had. I still think that she has followed my example and that makes me feel guilty somehow. I've never talked to her about my guilt though I've told her that I was sorry for her broken marriage and she knew that I had fixed my mistake, went back to my husband and remarried. She didn't follow in my steps, instead she married a divorced Englishman with an alcoholic problem.

    I am living the third age-role of my human life. It sounds funny as I write it because that language is used in science fiction movies, "human life" but it is real to express myself in that way because the next life is not human as we know it. If we are not inserted in the Body of Christ "via" Church, understanding these thoughts is not easy but very complicated. I remember that I used to express myself differently than I do now. How am I being changed into a different person or being? It is beyond my control and understanding and it is only because I am part of the Church, which is alive with life from above, that I am becoming a new creature and, according to the Holy Scriptures, His will is accomplished in me and done in me as it is being planned from the beginning of time that this transformation is possible and able to succeed. These transformations are being performed through the centuries to thousands of people; all those people who have been called to receive this new Spirit which is the Spirit of the Son of God named Jesus Christ by the archangel who announced His birth to His Holy mother, Mary of the house of David, the king. The same story is being told day after day to all the world by other "angels" (angel means messenger and everyone who is sent to spread the Good News, is one) In my case (I can only speak for myself) the way that I spread the news is by serving in the Mission and what is the mission? To do what I need to do, what I'm told, to go wherever I am needed when I'm needed and let me tell you that I need this Mission more that it needs me, because I need to take action in this magnificent adventure which is to live for the other, to work for the "Kingdom of Heaven" which it has started here on earth and it is going full speed and that as the Lord said: "My Kingdom is not of this world" and before that: "the Kingdom of Heaven is inside of you" to His disciples, those who were closer to Him. To live in this world like if you were not, those who are married as if they weren't, those who sale or buy as if they weren't, those who have properties as if they wouldn't have, etc. to enjoy everything as it is not ours, but it is ours because it belongs to our Father in Heaven who made everything for us. This is not a Philosophy or a spiritual Nirvana elevated language, but it is the Christian Way, and what it means is to prepare for the other life, the Eternal one, because we human beans are created in the image of God, He gives us His Spirit at the moment of birth (therefore the insistence of Mother Church to protect life and stop abortion) and that part of God's spirit must go back to Him because it is His. At the time of death, our soul lives in the body and travels towards eternity to meet its Maker, and whatever happened at that meeting we have all heard about would be according to that person's actions during his/her life here. And this is not easy to accept nor understand and we can't accept what we can't understand so that only by the Holy Spirit and the wisdom of the Church, we would come to believe such an outstanding fate. But the good news are that we all have a seed of faith implanted in us, an image of the truth so that deep inside we know that there is "something out there" and that sometimes we feel like we are immortals and we are but there is also the Gahanna the other side of Heaven which is what we should be trying very hard to avoid but not to forget.

St Agustin (the great Doctor of the Church) says in a discourse on the Psalms: "What then should the Christian do? He ought to use the world, not become its slave. And what does this mean? It means having, as though not having. He who is without anxiety waits without fear until his Lord comes. He will come whether we wish it or not. Do not think that because he is not coming right now, he will not come at all." He will come "St Agustin continues: "you know not when; and provided he finds you prepared, your ignorance of the time of his coming will not be held against you. Or do you, because you are unjust, expect the judge not to be just? Or because you are a liar, will the truthful one not be true?" For what have you that you have not received? (I'm quoting the Scriptures now) These are the sacrifices most pleasing to God: mercy, humility, praise, peace, charity. Such as these then, let us bring and, free from fear, we shall await the coming of the judge "who will judge the world in equity and the peoples in his truth." So, according to this great saint, Christ will come to judge and the end of the world, as we know it, its near, according to the signs of the times. So I have changed from that quiet little girl to a mature, Medicare recipient widow, and sometimes when I see myself in the mirror, I don't recognize the person in it.

Freso, CA

As my sons and I were getting ready to fly back home to California, we continue assisting to the celebrations of our small community and during one of this celebrations, one of my (catequistas) Charo, started talking to me asking me questions about when we were living and so and all of a sudden she looked at me and very seriously told me that I was to strive to have a Community in Fresno and from there, maybe help to make more in the Diocese which it has already happened. It took almost 5 years to start our Community and to do this, we received help from a sister whose name was Barbara who came to Fresno from her home town Riverside near Los Angeles. Her reasons to come to live in our town were strictly personal and I do not wish to use that information in the book but it was providential that she came and her help and dedication were extraordinary. Barbara was a soft spoken young German woman, a single mother of two boys. When we met her, her younger son Joshue was 2 or 3 years of age, a sharp blond blue-eyed toddler whom she would take everywhere. We, Carl, Barbara and I would visit the priests of the Dioceses, tell them our stories and offer the Way to (into) their parishes but the only parish that took us in was the Cathedral called St. John's because it has been dedicated, more than 100 years ago, to both saints: St. John the Baptist and St. John the Evangelist. We were so desperate to have the Community that we would pray together any chance we got. One Sunday, both families, she lived with her younger son and her mother and her older son John, already an adult, lived by himself outside of Fresno. So all of us decided to have a religious retreat so we took food, our bibles, our prayer books, our guitars and went to the city park and spent the day in prayer, singing the songs that we sing in Church, talking about the marvels God has done with us and our families, our visits to priests and the experiences that we have had in the Way. We had a great time and it was good for our souls to share and just be together like a mini- assembly on a Sunday. Our children played and laughed and Barbara and I sang songs together and got to know each other better. Later on, as we entered into the new Community we would always sit together because I used to translate for her (the Community was bilingual at the beginning) and she didn't know Spanish, also I bought a house a few blocks from her and we became neighbors which made our relationship even closer than before. We used to walk her dog through the neighborhood and shared ideas. After she became ill, I used to visit her and she was always hopeful and at peace with her fate. She prepared her last will and her funeral and she even left a song that she liked and asked for me to sing it during the service. She was my sister in Christ in every way and even now I pray for her intercession for the family and the Community and I missed her from the moment she passed away until this day. I am remembering her these days because Rosa Nelly's passing reminded me of her because both have been a great example of a Christian death for me and for many more people who knew them. Death in Church is a promise of Eternal Life and tears are transformed into laughter as one of the psalms said. You Lord will wipe every tear from your people's eyes and will take us out of the Pit of Death if we would only trust You for a second.

PARADISE

EXISTS!!!

Fresno, May 2011: About death and sin.

One day it will be my turn to go and it's all right, like the Beatles song says because now I've received the Message of Salvation and I have hope that Heaven exists and somehow I've felt Eternity even for a split second (of a second) and because of that I know that there is life after death, yes the big dilemma has been resolved for me and for many members of the small communities that there are appearing in the Church everywhere. That thought being carried in my mind and in my soul, makes all the difference. Man is afraid of death ontologically suffers from the "fear of death" and that fear slave us to sin. To sin is to go against God and to make wrong choices, freely and with a full intention of the will to go against the Will of God. It is not to eat the famous apple as most of the people think, anyhow sin has to do with that event in Paradise when Adam and Eve his companion, disobey the order not to eat from the tree of knowledge situated in a special place in the Garden of Eden and that "wrong choice of the will" (their will) started the downfall of Humanity as we know it. Is it a children's night story? Serpent and all….? Or is it the beginning of sin, whose father is The Devil, to spread as the bad seed throughout all the World? I think that the Holy Scriptures contained the truth and that is the way that happened, and to me it makes sense and even I've been told that there are other versions of it (the Bible speaks of two) I go for the first one written in the Book of Genesis because God can create anything. He sets His power to (into) from any material He chooses, whenever He decides to do it and anywhere He pleases. So there that is the answer, simple, uncomplicated and to the point. He placed the perfect couple to live in the perfect place and forever. The fact that the couple decided to do their will to "become like Him?" made the difference and there are consequences to our mistakes and to the wrongs that we do, even if it's done unintentionally. The typical expression "sorry" may be good enough when we step on someone's toe, but to have to say it constantly and for the same mistakes, it's not good. When we confess our sins (and even in the Scriptures) when the adulterous the woman was delivered by Jesus from being stoned to death, He looked at her and told her: "Go and sin no more" and that was more an order (done in a very tender way) than a request. I read somewhere that " Love means never having to say Sorry" and it is an intelligent thought. The "passing" of our sister Rosa Nelly has placed a fix word in my mind: One day I will be in a nice looking pastel color coffin and my soul will go in from of the trial Court of the afterlife and I'm not trying to scare anybody but it is what comes to my mind more often than before she went away and it helps because "it's the thought that counts" and if it keeps me from sinning and walking closer and closer to the place kept for me in Heaven, the better. I need all the help I can get and I pray to all those who have gone before me to intercede for me in front of The Father that I would join them when my turn comes.

Fresno, CA 2011: About the heart of the Church:

Today, the 1st of October, The Church celebrates the Memorial of one of its Doctors St. Teresa of the Child Jesus also known as Teresa of Lisieux, a town in France. And I wanted to copy a few paragraphs of her Biography: "When I had looked upon the mystical body of the Church, I recognized myself in none of the members which Saint Paul described, and what is more, I desired to distinguish myself more favorably within the whole body. Love appeared to me to be the hinge for my vocation. Indeed, I knew that the Church had a body composed of various members, but in this body the necessary and more noble member was not lacking; I knew that the Church had a heart and that such a heart appeared to be aflame with love. I knew that one love drove the members of the Church to action, that if this love were extinguished, the apostles would have proclaimed the Gospel no longer, the martyrs would have shed their blood no more. I saw and realized that love sets off the bounds of all vocations, that love is everything, that this same love embraces every time and every place. In one word, that love is everlasting. Then, nearly ecstatic with the supreme joy in my soul, I proclaimed: O Jesus, my love, at last I have found my calling: my call is love. Certainly I have found my proper place in the Church, and you gave me that very place, my God. In the heart of the Church, my mother, I will be love, and thus I will be all things, as my desire finds its direction." That piece appears on Volume IV of The Liturgy of the Hours in the second reading of the Office of Readings page 1450 of the 1975 edition Catholic Book Publishing Co. New York, N.Y. When I prayed the morning prayer and read this beautiful passage my thoughts were to place it as the heading of this page because this saint is special not only she is one of the few women nominated Doctors of the Church, but also she was a Carmelite nun at a very young age, suffered much opposition from her family and her congregation, became ill during the few years that she lived in the convent, embraced poverty, chastity, the very chilled nights of the north of France and she gave her short life to Jesus because she loved Him and she wanted to give her love to Him completely and unlimited. She knew the Church had a heart and she wanted to be in the center of it. I also liked this piece in which she talks about the Church having a body composed of various members which is what I've been trying to explain in some parts of the book. It is important to know this because that is the reason why the Church is called to be an assembly (Church = Assembly) Iglesia in Spanish Ecclesia from Latin Reunion-Assembly and every one of its members has a place and a role in a particular personal space within this special body. It makes a lot of sense then that the Church needs to reunite to form this body and the Head (Jesus) takes over the body and there is a presence (through the Holy Spirit) in the Assembly being formed by the members who have been summoned to attend the Liturgical Celebration of the moment. In a Church Community everybody' presence is accepted and welcomed as an important part of the body. Treatment should be equal, the service must be done with respect and the Priest represents Christ and that is why he sits at the head of the assembly presiding the celebration. It takes time to learn the roll of the Church and it's people into the world but it is arranged that way since the beginning by the Apostles and later on it's been cared for the descendants of these first disciples and Apostles and the (Jerarquia) has a perfect explanation in every personal case.

CHRISTIANITY IS NOT A PHILOSOPHY

Fresno, CA May 2011

Christianity is not a philosophy nor a doctrine or even a religion; no, Christianity is a Way of Life. If you are a Christian you are like-Christ or another Christ and you have Eternal Life in you and live differently. You could most probably make miracles and behave as if your head was in Heaven and your feet on earth. I wish I could explain myself better, but it is not easy to put words to a particular "way of life". I am writing about a whole life being different sometimes even from birth. When a person is born in a Christian family it is educated as a Christian, to have the knowledge of God first of all followed by being baptized into the bosom of Mother Church, received all the sacraments which comes after baptism, and by the power of the Holy Spirit becomes an adult Christian having all the responsibilities and (privilegios) of being a child of God. If a person doesn't believe in God nor Jesus Christ and by being given the Message of Salvation, accepts it and becomes a member of The Church, like I did, then this person or persons are instructed in the knowledge of the truth and are called catechumens. If this person/s decides to follow Jesus and obey the Commandments could be a disciple and on the right time, he/she could be apostles, messengers, missionaries, presbyters or/and bishops, deacons, seminarians, lectors, cantors, nuns, novices, altar servers, acolitos and any other place or service the Church needs at the moment that the candidate or neophyte enters or responds to the call to be a Christian. God is in history, He makes History and He is also in our history so if we get to experience this, and decide to accept it, He would help us to have a history, a true history and a good one. When I became a catechumen I didn't know very well what was all about, the people around me were different, the liturgical celebrations were beautiful but also different. I used to go to mass with my grandmother when I started to live with her and I was just there with her but my heart wasn't. I remember thinking that every word said during the Mass was said in Latin, the priest was looking ahead giving his back to the congregation and the altar boys (there were no altar girls yet) will answer the priest and ring the bell from time to time. I didn't get any of it then, even though when I was in the (Internado) nun's school, all the students would go to Mass every morning before breakfast, receive communion, have confessions, pray the rosary, listen to Missions every lent season and all of us were educated into the Catholic-Christian doctrine. I used to be very pious and devout and I remember even praying to a statue of Our Mother with real intensity and maybe even she would answer me. The whole experience during the time I spent at that School was strong and meaningful and I had a kind of a secret admired who was the son of the gardeners who would sing songs at night under my bedroom window and I think that the nuns found out because I was moved to a far east window where it was impossible for anybody to get my attention. I am saying this because if the nuns found out they never said anything to me. This boy, the son of the gardener as we used to call him, would if possible send me love notes which I've read carefully and make disappear as soon as I've read them. I am writing as I remember moments of my life and as I do this, I make comparisons in my mind about how I acted before and after my Encounter with Jesus and His Church. Christianity is a way of Life and anybody might be called to become one in many different ways, and only God does the calling on His own terms and when He wants. I've already told my experience but my sister

Philly 08/17/2015

O my soul. Created to enjoy such exquisite gifts, what are you doing? Where is your life going? How wretched is the blindness of Adam's children, if indeed we are blind to such a brilliant light and deaf to so insistent a voice. (From a Spiritual Canticle by st. John of the Cross) -second reading 18th week in ordinary time – Volume IV-

To be able to understand our need and rights to get to know God, the true God- it's necessary to take a journey to the past of Humanity (our own past) How life was from the beginning… and the story-our story- on the Bible. The story in the Bible starts like that: "In the beginning there was ..." etc. study, learn the people's customs, how they thought, their laws, why the idols, sacrifices to their idols, their needs, why the rites (some of them we also have now) altars made with stones (the stone which the builders rejected, has become the corner stone) refers to Jesus son of the true God.

This is what, if men want to know God, the God of Abraham, Isaac and Jacob, must read the Bible, the books that teach about Him. Needs to be close to the Word "In the beginning there was the Word and the Word was God". "I am the Way, the Truth and the Life". Men need to understand the reason for the Church (Assembly) among us, reachable and yet too far if we are not called to be part of it, a member of His body. Why the hunger, the need to feel loved, wanted by somebody. Why the search for the truth? Fear of the Lord is the beginning of wisdom. The book of Wisdom is part of the Bible together with many more, particularly the Acts of the apostles were men who are searching, looking for answers, may find the way that some church members had been following the Mission which Jesus gave them: Go and tell others even to all the nations, about me, tell them that the Kingdom of Heaven is at hand, near, even inside of us, inside of men. Those who listen and believe will be saved!. What do I need to be saved from? "Come to me those we are thirsty, or hungry that I will fill you up."

Once, a few weeks ago, while watching a program, one of those "make believed Court real cases" and, after the case was over, the chairperson of the program, the "judge" read a phrase from the late and very much missed Indira Gandhi which goes something like this: "It is a privilege to live an extraordinary life with it's lot of misfortune and difficulties" and that was a consolation to me because I've lived an extraordinary life full of sorrows and disappointments and I still am. That wise saying lifted up my burden of that particular day.

Good for Miss Ghandi! I am trying through these pages to tell the story of my life which might seem a long one but it has been really short. The Book of Psalms said that men lived to be 70 years or 80 if there is strong vigor in his body. It is in reference to modern men because men during the time of the Old Testament (before it was even written) lived more than 100 years -standard age- many people, according to The Bible lived over 300 years or more. Our Patriarch Abraham for example and his wife Sarah were already old (according to our standards) when they conceived their first child Isaac and lived many years to raise their son to an adult age. Moses also lived to be very old and Noah too. So God decided that after the fall, men would live a shorter life as a way to prevent them from acting against Him and each other for a very long time. I hope that I am explaining myself because I'm really trying. At this moment of my life, I can look back calmly and remember how I was when I was a young girl, walking with my sisters around the corner from our large house up a hilly street to school which was a short distance for children our age. I had a "normal" childhood, never doing anything to be discussed with my father over dinner (even though I don't remember any dinners at any table) . I suppose that I would do my homework, listen to the teachers, go to the Principal's Office sometimes and so on. We had an aunt, the older sister of my father's, her name was Ramona and she had beautiful clear eyes which resembled a big cat or even a mountain lion. She was a seamstress and used to see pretty dresses for us, my sisters and I. My younger sister Angela was her godchild and she would pay more attention to her and we all knew it and accepted. She was also a little on the heavy side and baked fantastic lemon cakes which my sisters and I would devour as soon as she would put a piece on our plate. I do not remember my other father's sisters (I believe she had 3) very much. Perhaps another older sister Magdalena who had a large house which she used as a Pension, the Spanish word for a Bed & Breakfast Inn, which she will manage, helped by her two daughters, our cousins whom I do remember, were very nice to us and always treated us with kindness and love. That is one of the reasons for which I think my father as a nice man, who used to drink alcohol and maybe was an alcoholic and my brain has erase the bad memories from my mind as a what it is known today as a defense mechanism which hides parts of our memory when necessary to protect us from excessive stress and pain.

It is very hard to admit an illness and this weakness stays with you for the rest of your life. After Thanksgiving 2010 and the first episode where my heart lost its rhythmic rate and I suffered from Atrial Fibrillation. I was at my son's parish celebrating the days of the feast of Thanksgiving when I started getting sick and after a while my son and my sister who had come to spend that special day with her husband decided to take me to a nearby clinic. I stayed there in the cardiac unit for three days until one of the doctors, after performing several tests on me, decided to apply an Electroshock to control the erratic biting of my heart. The fourth day I was prepared and taken to surgery and after I had been put under, it was done. My son C. accompanied me during the procedure and my sister and brother in law waited for him. Their company was a balsam for my soul and I understood why Jesus Christ made visiting the sick into one work of Mercies. I don't know what I would have done if I would've been by myself during this difficult time. Thank God that He has given me a family that loves me and cares. When I came up from the anesthesia, I felt good that I was still alive and at that moment, the doctor told me that everything had been done well and that my heart was back to "normal". I was back at my son's that same day but my sister and brother in law had to be at their parish so we all left together; a brother from my son's community volunteered to drive us home, so we went. I was still feeling a little weak but happy that my heart was biting the way that it was supposed to bite even though the cardiologist who had performed the procedure told me to see my doctor as soon as possible because I had a damaged valve and it needed immediate attention. The situation was very serious and as soon as I was back in N.J. I took care of it, went to my doctor and started to talk about the surgery and probably an implant. After performing more tests and evaluations, I was prescribed some nuclear medicine and the surgery was arranged for March 1st, a date which I accepted because it sounded right for everybody and the preparations started right away. The Lord kept me calm and joyful even though I knew the risks of such surgery. The husband of one of The sisters from my Church Community had the same valve repair not transplanted and it seemed to me that his case was easier than mine. Anyways, I talked to this couple and learned a little about my valve problem and I knew right away that the implant had to be done or I could die sooner than expected or have more complications or a heart attack if I'd survived these. The ordeal of the surgery, the Hospital, the preparations, the tests, etc. were excruciating and I went along assisted by The Holy Spirit and His strength all the way.

I look at myself now and I do not recognize that person, the new person whom God is creating. God is recreating me, making a new creation, something very difficult to accept. It is one of those concepts that we might have heard, maybe even understand in a philological manner or just as something that we have heard while going to college or perhaps had read in a serious volume in a nearby Library. I am talking in an existential response, a real one. One time I was a person that couldn't love and accept my husband, did not understand the vice of alcohol that has been in the family genes perhaps for several generations, a woman looking for her own happiness and well being blind to anything outside herself and her immediate basic needs. Unable to think about someone else's happiness and capable of doing whatever necessary to do my will, my plan no matter what. While listening to the catequesis in Church, I heard many truths and vital facts and one of the concepts that (which) convinced me the most was that men without God's Spirit react on that same way as I was acting and that it is expected because men (the old man) Adam's descendents, are condemned to act like that and to commit the same selfish acts over and over until he/she is redeemed, changed (converted) and announced the Good News (The Gospel) to. Only in that way, Jesus Christ can come to our lives, show us what He did for us (dying He conquered Death and free us from the curse which the evil one put on us through sin. As always, all these are hard to explain and I believe that perhaps it is even pure Theology which I do not know anything about. All I can tell is my experience, what my encounter with the son of God meant for me and for my family because even though not everybody in the family had heard the Good News (the message of Salvation) or had heard it and rejected -like some of them did- my so called invitation to convert, has touched every member of the family, some more than others and there are facts which shows these positive changes making even now changes in every one's history and their life realities. Changes which had caused a powerful movement which invisible waves still shakes the waters of life that like a river touches everything and provides new life washing old behaviors and old habits and awakening the consciences of all the members of the family and everyone which comes in contact with any of us.

Fresno, 11/22/2015 Christ The King- Today while waiting for the bus, I told a young man who was also at the Bus-stop, that this Sunday the Church celebrates that very important feast and as he was listening, I asked him if he believed in God he told me that he was Catholic and took the opportunity to tell him that I just been in Church and that at the end of it, the priest always tells the Congregation to go and share the Good News (Gospel) now that we had celebrated. Then I explained to this young man that it's what I was doing, passing on the message from the Church to him. I think that he was impressed by my answer and smiled while continuing to pay attention to my words. I told him that it was not easy to understand that Christ died for all of us a terrible and cruel death which He accepted freely taking our place as men (us) committed the first sin by disobeying the advice of God in Paradise. I explained carefully that only by faith is possible to believe; While the Word is being preached to us in the Assembly, the Holy Spirit (the third person of the Holy Trinity) also a Mystery, seals in our hearts (souls) the truth and that is the way the Church teaches Her Doctrine. After I said that, he seemed to accept the explanation and told me that he had learnt a lot about Christ and His Church. I told him that I was glad and then the bus arrived.

Fresno 11/17/2015 - Christians who wish to escape the rigor of Purgatory must love the mortification of their Divine Master, and beware of being delicate members under a head crowned with thorns. On February 10, 1656 in the province of Lyons, father Francis of Aix, of the Society of Jesus, passed away to a better life. He carried all virtues of a Religious to a high degree of perfection. Penetrated with a profound veneration towards the Most Blessed Trinity, he had for particular intention in all his prayers and mortifications, to honor this August Mystery; to embrace by preference those works for which others showed less inclination, had a particular charm for him. He often visited the Blessed Sacrament, even during the night, and never left the door of his room without going to say a prayer at the foot of the altar. His penances, which were in a manner excessive, gave him the name of "The man of suffering". Another fault against which we must guard, because we so easily fall into it, is the mortification of the tongue, Oh! How easy it is to err in words! How rare a thing it is to speak for any length of time without offending meekness, humility, sincerity or Christian Charity! Even pious persons are often subject to this defect; when they have escaped all the other snares of the demon, they allow themselves to be taken, says St. Jerome, in this last trap-slander-. Everything we do, how we act and/or respond, has its consequences which may lead us to make more serious mistakes, errors and even grave sins. The Church, our Mother (The Mother of Jesus) teaches what to do to choose Heaven, but first we must be directed towards It as we are passing through enemy territory and taking the wrong route can be dangerous and fatal. Christians who are convinced of such Mystery being true, will be attacked with more fury than they expect and would need to take refuge under the protection of our Savior who is always waiting for us to ask. "Ask and shall be given to you" pure and simple put into words by the Master Himself. Just ask, He is telling us even to the point of making this advice easier for anyone, He says: "when two or more are reunited in my name, ask and everything will be given to you".

Marxism had the illusion that social justice and the globalization of the economy would solve the problems that were encountered in those times. That illusion has vanished. "The poor need justice not Charity!" Marx exclaimed in this new doctrine. The Church social justice, as the perfect expression of Christian Faith, "Give to Caesar what is Caesar and to God what is God's" has revolutionized the world and the forgiveness of sins had liberated man from slavery, not just by not having a master but by being given the possibility of becoming a child of God, another Christ.

SilverSpring, MD 07/18/2013

After being an itinerant-missionary (any person in Church willing to be sent anywhere to serve in Parishes or Seminaries), my life changed enormously for the better, towards my relationship with Christ, my relations with my family, friends and the brothers and sisters of the small Christian Communities which have been forming in several places with the inspiration of the Holy Spirit. People around me seemed to have another mentality after I became one of the many members of the neo-catechumen ate (an Itinerary of Faith to help us to rediscover our Baptism) . I have mentioned this in another chapter. In this town I'm living in a big and comfortable house with another missionary and we're both serving in the same Parish about 20 minutes away. The house owner who also lives in the house tries very hard to please us and keep us happy. So, at the moment I'm sharing my life with these women who are believers and members of the Church. My room-mate and I participate as much as possible in the new Evangelization propose by pope Francis who is very much for the changes promoted by the Vatican II Council and in friendly terms with the founders of "The Way" which is the name given to this Itinerary of Faith, so welcomed by any bishop that is aware of the crisis taking over the Church everywhere. In the year 2013 declared "The Year of Faith" by pope Francis, two of my grandsons assisted to the "World Youth Day" meeting, organized in Rio de Janeiro, Brazil and there the pope and Joseph's team asked the Church to announced the Gospel from every corner of the globe which have beginning to be done also with the help and inspiration of the Holy Spirit alive in His Church and it has been done with great enthusiasm and joy.

From the Kerygma in the shantytown with the poor: Joseph Albiro – About marriage and family: When one puts all his being in the love of a woman that he feels loved by, and that woman falls in love

With another man and leaves him; that man experiences in himself something that he did not know: hell. Immediately he experiences within himself a horror, an abyss is opened before him: he goes from being to not being; he does not exist, and experiences total darkness. This suffering is so great that he asks himself: "How can I make my wife understand the harm, the tremendous evil that she has done to me? And thinks…: "killing the children!"

Something like this made my husband feel when I let him. Alone and abandoned. Every four (4) minutes a marriage is broken in Spain and in Italy. I live in the USA now and don't have the exact figures in this country, but I know that divorce is like a plague hunting every marriage. Some of the members of my family are separated or divorce, some are not seeking marriage in Church. I don't blame them nor judge them because they don't know any better. Maybe they went to Mass when young or had received the sacraments, made their first communion, etc, but in a particular moment of their lives, stopped going and receiving the sacraments or /and going to Mass even on Sundays. The prince of this world is waiting as long as it needs to trap us, deceives us and takes our souls from God. He hates us because he knows that we have the possibility to be saved and go to Heaven and he hasn't. He, the evil one, has no hope, The Lord has other plans for him. Beware of his presence and of his power. God allows him to tent us so that we will learn to turn towards Him and beg him "not to let us fall into temptation but deliver us from evil" (part of the prayer that Jesus taught his disciples, "the Our Father"). Why did I leave my husband? He was a hard worker, responsible to his job and to his family. Quite charming, friendly, honest to the Air Force, proud to be a soldier, to be an American. Born in Texas, educated in a Catholic school, in love with me, happy to be a father of two handsome boys, etc. Well, I left him because in my opinion he drank too much, and after drinking, I would be very upset and angry and I would stop talking to him for what he would consider a long time. I would refuse to have any kind of intimacy with him and treated him badly and sometimes even rude. I believe that made him become angry also and the bottle became his first love. Military life is lonely and hard, even though military bases have all the facilities families might need. I tried to make it happy for me and all of us, even when the Air Force stationed him in a Base in Rapid City, SD a harsh and cold place. The devil had already harvested a seed of hatred towards my husband. By the end of our first year there, I was ready to leave. My husband. Carl was already suspicious of me leaving him so when I told him that I was to go visit my family for a while, he told me that I could only take one of the kids with me. I took the older one, Chris, to Spain. Everything seemed ok in the beginning but after some time there, I began to miss my other son, Michael, so I came back.

After that, our relationship took another turn and I felt resentment towards him because of the mistrust he had on me. Things started to change rapidly and we became bitter towards each other and the marriage didn't work. Now I know why. Even though we had the sacrament, we were unaware of it and never turned to God or the

Church for help. We were outsiders. The situation was very difficult and we didn't have a chance to make it work by ourselves. I left again when Ray was stationed in Germany. I thought then that was my last chance to run away from it all.

The Catechism of the Catholic Church says that original sin has wounded man. We are wounded! What does this mean? All of us know that to love, to help those in need, to participate in good works of mercy, to help the poor, etc is beautiful. But then we find another reality, a profound one "when I want to do what it's right, then, like St. Paul says!"

Something extraordinary happened on the day that the Catequesis (the announcement of salvation) which saved my life, started. I was still at my brother's home, I think that I was there for maybe two years (2), and I was getting ready to go and listen because my brother and others had put all their hopes in this changing the direction of my life and I've also wanted to see what this was all about because I have been invited to a few celebrations in the Church Community and I had already seen something different in these people because they'd talk about God entering in their lives and changing them and as they knew Him in a very intimate way. Anyhow, I was waiting for a friend of the family, a woman, who had also been invited to listen. She had been divorced for several years, had 6 grown children and according to people who knew her well, she has been feeling kind of down for some time. It was getting close to the time of the meeting when my most recent boyfriend entered in the kitchen looking for me and when he saw me all dressed up he asked me where was I going and I said that I was going to church to listen to a very important announcement, then he opened a paper bag that he was carrying and showed me a lot of money and semi covered by the money, a small gun. As soon as I saw the money he looked intensely at me and said that if I come with him right away he'll take me to a nice place in the country (he knew some people who lived in a small town near Madrid), we could had a lot of fun, he continued and take a few trips to relax and be together. Immediately, I felt excited about the trip and the money but something inside made me hesitate and I waited even though I could see that he was getting frustrated and was in a hurry to go (he was anxious because of the gun and I knew that he wasn't used to having contact with one). The moment was tense, the timing not too convincing and my brother came down stairs and saw us together. Immediately, he looked at me and with a serious expression on his face told me that if I did go with my friend instead of going to the Catequesis, I would be sorry for the rest of my life. At that point, I knew that I had to help him to get rid of the gun and he wasn't planning on living it behind, so I decided to go with him to a nearby park which had a good size lake and since my plan was to throw the gun into the water, we rented a boat, made my friend row to the middle of the lake and ask him to put the gun in. He didn't argue and did it. At that minute I felt relieved and asked him to take me back to my brothers because I was going to Church and my family's friend was picking me up very shortly after taking the boat back to shore, we took a taxi and went to wait for her. When we got there, she was already waiting because my brother had told her what had happened, so I turned towards my boyfriend (he was going to be only a friend from that day on) and went to listen to the message that God had prepared for me on that particular day. Sometimes I think about what would've happened if I would have gone with him instead of to church and I feel so good that I didn't go. I am also very thankful to my brother for his support because the words that came out of his mouth helped me to make the right choice. May God Bless him and help him to come back to Church because he has been away for sometime now and he needs to have God in his life again and he knows it, but that is another chapter of the story. I think that it's been said already that the friend who wanted to take me away from Church on that day, is now in a Church Community, is married to a Christian woman and, the last time I saw him, he was the father of 5 beautiful children. I think that I didn't mention that the day that he went looking for me, he had stolen the money somewhere and that is why he was carrying that gun which is now at the bottom of the lake covered with sand.

During the early 60's as Spain continued recuperating from the great 50's changes which were already starting in the rest of Europe and trying to rise to the European standards of comfort, God started a renewal nobody was aware of. Pope John XXIII begin to organize the II Vatican Council which would produced an spiritual awareness very much needed throughout the Universal Church and there was a man (*still is) who was looking for answers, the same answers which everybody is looking for with more or less intensity. His name is Francisco Arguello and he was a famous artist, a painter, very well known in Madrid, Spain and a disciple of the great Picasso. While listening to a documentary about Pope John XXIII, he heard the Pope said something that called to his attention that "You who are looking for Jesus could find Him among the poor" this same expression was probably put into the inner place of Teresa of Calcutta's heart and she also started to live among the poorest of the poor on the suburbs of India and by doing this humble service, found meaning for her life and the Love who surpasses all understanding. So our hero Joseph left his treasures behind, his family, a comfortable home (he belongs to a wealthy and bourgeois family) and all his friends and followers, and went to live in an area in the outbursts of Madrid were gipsy like people, delinquents of all kind, prostitutes and all those rejected by society looked for a place to live because they do not find it anywhere else. Francisco made his own "whole in the wall" and to survived, started to teach in a public school near by and begin to make contact with his neighbors and pretty fast he had made a group of friends whom would come to ask him questions about the Bible (he will always carry one with him) and what he was doing there, question which he would answered gladly and honestly. Little by little, the group was being form by the Holy Spirit into a small Christian Community something which Joseph didn't expected nor lest he had any idea it would happened but it did and he started slowly and with great care to cultivate and allowing the Spirit to grow and lead, the reality of the Church, presented in front of him and in his eagerness to find The Lord, he accepted the Miracle which it's later mentioned in the Catequesis, that when the "Moral Miracle" appears, the Church's Mission is accomplished and when we let God take control of our lives, things can become right again. It doesn't mean that problems are going to disappear but we would not be alone in the battle anymore and if the will of God is done (as we ask in the Our Father) then His creations (meaning also us) would be made anew and in harmony all.

After my reconciliation with my husband approximately in Fall of 1983, early fall or end of summer, I started to prepare for our trip (my two sons and myself) back to California. I remember that it was a happy time and the children were excited and eager to come back though I knew that they'd worry about the future and that thinking about being with their father again caused them sorrow and stress but I told them to trust in The Lord and that The Church will be there to help us, something that helped them both immensely and the fact that we'd go to the celebration of the Word with our Church Community made everything easier. Chris is older and he could take more responsibility for his actions and I also noticed that he'd remembered my husband better than his brother who was more uneasy than him. Anyhow, I think that God made the time go faster than usual and soon we were ready to go back all the time, putting our future in His hands. The company where I worked for almost a year decided to give me a farewell check to compensate me for the vacation time which I did not use and with that money I purchased the plane tickets. On the day of the trip, we said our goodbyes to the family and took a cub to Barajas which was then I think half the size of the actual one. On the other hand, even though it was much smaller, there was more security and there was even a small police station situated just before the entrance to the Gates. It was there, at this small station that one of the biggest miracles of my life took place and I had talked about it many times over as a strong testimony of what God has done for me. The Chief of police had been notified by the agent who checked our passports that there had been an error in our traveling papers. My son's names were in my Spanish passport but the time spent in Spain has been more than they were allowed as US citizens and he did not let them go without first being registered at one of the Embassies of their country. I was shocked by this news and I told him that I didn't know about this legal problem and that it was my fault and that I was very sorry and while I was saying this to him my tears started rolling down my face and I started to beg to please let us go…..The relative of one of the sisters of our Church Community, decided to accompany us to the Gate and when he saw what was happening, and since he knew the chief of police very well, started also begging him (by his first name) to let us go and all the time telling him the story of our sudden reconciliation after almost 4 years being divorced. Many workers of the airport started listening to us and waited for the result of such controversy (in suspense) While all this was going on, the Chief of Police named Pepe, gave one of the agents instructions to take us to the US Embassy and at that point, he turned to me and with a surprised expression in his face, told him to take us to the plain instead…I couldn't believe what I saw as my sister's relative getting close to me murmured: "never forget that today God has opened the sea for you!" We started walking towards the exit gate and many followed saying goodbye and showing their support to us. I shall add that the crew of our plane waited by the open door nearly 10 minutes and the look of welcomed which they gave us was like an injection of the positive energy needed to start Back to the Future, the movie which we saw later on when we got home and that helped my sons and I to understand better what God has prepared for us.

I've finally become old like I've wanted to so many times…..

Of all the victims that we (the world) offers to it's God or gods every day In suffering persecution resides the probe of the truth (La persecución me convence de la verdad)

Gracias a la persecución me convenzo cada vez más de que Cristo ha resucitado Y de que hay un Dios creador y magnánimo que hace y ha hecho desde siempre, Una historia de salvación con la humanidad que Él mismo creó para que experimentaran en toda su plenitud al misterio de la vida y compartiéramos Con Él la creación entera y Su gran amor….

Three important vital questions Humanity asks: who am I? Why am I here? And Where am I going? The finger of God points towards the thinking man and beyond That to what?

Answer: It points to the same direction because when a man's life has no meaning, either his world is a "tragic trap" in which he lives without hopes and dies without dignity or as Teilard de Chardin wrote many years ago, a great becoming…in which mankind is thrust towards a glorious completion in Christ. I believe there is a Plan of completion for the future union of the church with Christ. This completion has Very little or nothing to do with the eternal plan of God.

Baptism page 2 (about the need to receive the sacrament of Baptism)

We who have been reborn (in the Spirit) through the sacrament of baptism experience intense joy when we feel within us the first stirrings of the Holy Spirit. We begin to have an insight into the mysteries of faith, we are able then to prophesy and to speak with wisdom. We become steadfast in hope and receive the gift of healing. Demons are made subject to the authority of the children (sons of God) These gifts enter us like a gentle rain, and, once having done so, little by little, they bring forth fruit in abundance.

Baptism has been and still is the entrance to the correspondence Assembly wherever denomination. but Baptism as a sacrament (sacred) was established through the Institution of the Church with St Peter as the head of it. We need to go back to the times of the first sending of some of the disciples, as apostles to the Mission "Go and announce that the Kingdom of Heaven is near." Our Lord Jesus entered into the waters of the river Jordan to be baptized by his cousin John and after that, went into the desert to begin his preparation for the announcing of the Kingdom of God. So it is true that John prepared the way for his coming as it was expected and written by the prophets from the beginning of time. In the beginning was The Word and The Word was God. The second person of the Holy Trinity.

As it can be seen, Faith is vital and absolutely necessary for the Mission of the Christians, and only, while receiving the Faith, and only then, they would be able to evangelize (we the Christians) The Jew Nation are the closest to all the other (churches) – denominations- not only for their roots but because our Lord is their Messiah Joshue. The disciples started preaching the Gospel (Good News) in Jerusalem (Esteban first martyr) while he was talking about Jesus (the Messiah) according to the law of Moses.

On Baptism (catechesis of Pope Paul VI) General Audience to the Neocatechumenal Way 12/01/1977)

To be able to understand our need and right to be baptized, to get to know God, uit is necessary to take a journey to the past of Humanity – our own past- How life was from the beginning, the story of the Bible, the stories of lives in the Bible. On of the first books of the Bible starts like this: 'In the beginning the was… Therefore, we need to learn the people's customs, their thoughts, laws and why, idols, the meaning and need for sacrifices, the rites, conduct, the reasons they had for altars, offerings and such.

Christ was baptized as an adult but presented in the Temple as a child, even a newborn. What were the rights of the first born, and even now in our days, we baptize our children while they're still babies.

St Augustine says: "If we cannot have the Catechumenate beforehand, we'll carry it out afterwards. That is, the instruction, completion and education, the whole of the Church's education work, after Baptism. Pope Paul VI says in his catechesis on Baptism that: "The sacrament of Christian regeneration must once again return to being what it was in the consciousness and custom of the first generation of Christians and the first norms of the Church." When we baptize the newly born, what instruction do they receive? It is necessary therefore that the godparents speak on its behalf. But the latter does not benefit from the testimony given by the godparents to the priest. The word catechumenate refers to baptism. It was the period of preparation for baptism. Nowadays, baptism does not have the same development, at least in its didactic preparation. The Neocatechuments, our visitors today say: "We will carry out this preparation after baptism. The sanctifying grace of this sacrament received was not sufficient, on the contrary, this grace has lighted a fire which needs to spread into the whole of the baptized person's life.

Before, during the early times (40's and 50's) the period of preparation or catechumenate was limited to a condense and ritualistic time of education because all families were Catholic, were good, everybody was Christian and children were expected to learn along the way mostly in Catholic schools. Today our society is no longer

This is the proof that we remain in him and he in us, that he has given us a share in his Spirit. We ourselves have seen and testify that the Father sent his son as savior of the world. Anyone who acknowledges that Jesus is the son of God, God remains in him and he in God. We have recognized for ourselves and put our faith in the love God has for us. God is love, and whoever remains in Love remains in God and God in him. This is one of the cores (columna) of Christianity; a very profound, very deep truth which explains and teaches the special Relationship we have with God and with each other as His Church. The apostles are saying that they testify that the Father sent his Son as savior of The World and why would The

World need a savior? The question implies a situation of slavery, imprisonment or danger, and it is because when The Lord called me to His Church to listen to the Message of Salvation, the moment I heard it, I knew that I've been saved and later on as I kept coming to listen in the Assembly, little by little I realized from how many dangers and errors I was taken from and, for the first time in years of struggle and suffering, I felt relieved and joyful and I thought to myself that I have found what I have been looking all my life. I have found LOVE capital letters Love and I relaxed. I was given proof that the words above are true and that I and all those people present, as they believed, had received a share in His Spirit. God gathered us in that parish to give us His Spirit through the preaching of The Gospel as promised to the disciples from the beginning and also through the Prophets whom He also called to a Mission, and everyone on different times in history and during diverse circumstances and the needs of His chosen people, the descendents of Israel, first called Jacob. I learnt later on that my family, my ancestors, have been Jews and probably from the tribe of Judah but I didn't have any idea then that I would be called, first because I was suffering, alone and in need and also because of my bloodline. The world is suffering because it does not know God and people walk around like zombies trying to get relief for their anguish which would not stop until our soul rests in God. God put in men the need/wish to see His face says Pope Benedict XVI, and we wouldn't see it unless we answer His calling when it is our turn to be called. God looked for the lost sheep and He found me because I was that lost sheep and He knew that I would answer to His calling because I was lost and I knew it and that is the beautiful thing about it that He has a plan and it is to save Humanity, all of it, all of us and then, if we want, He'd give us the Spirit of His only son and make us Christians (like Christ) In my situation, I am following on the steps of Jesus as accurately as I can and always guided by the light of the Church, while being sustained by the Sacraments as I've explained earlier in this book. I have sinned and hurt people, rejected the love of friends, my husband's and members of my family and, although I was unconscious of my actions, I still hurt them and destroyed many relations which God had put in my life to love and cherish and care for and lied to them and despised them and didn't love them back. The world would say that I was right, that I was taking care of my needs and that I am free to do with my body what I want but, it is not so and I've experienced death and bitterness and a longing for love beyond anything imaginable. God put an end to my misery the only way which is planned to be done, and it is having the Good Shepherd guide me back into His bosom, Mother Church. There is suffering in doing the will of God but that is the only life I can have and the only way out of myself into Rightness and true happiness.

THE MISSION

The first time that I stood up as a volunteer to go on a Mission, I answered to an invitation to serve the Church as an "itinerant" which means to be able to go anywhere, anytime, to do anything as a service to the needs of others. As the Catechists were asking, my heart was pounding and I stood up trembling but happy to do it. Unfortunately my husband didn't respond the same way and he remained seated comfortably on the chair next to mine. He just looked at me waiting not knowing what to do. Carl was not aware of the procedure because he hasn't been called to the Community yet. He came to the retreat that day to be with me and take me back home. He didn't say anything though and I felt the need to talk to a priest who was a friend of mine to ask for advice, he told me that I needed to wait for my husband and our sons to be ready to go also and at that moment, I realized that I've been wrong and impulsive to volunteer without talking to my family first and I didn't say another word. I don't think that we mentioned the possibility of being an "itinerant family" . We never talked about it and I was fine with that, it just wasn't meant to be. My friend the priest told me though that the important thing was that God saw me standing up and that was all. I kept that thought with me all those years until, after I became a widow I decided to dedicate my time to be a missionary and serve the Church and from that moment on I stood and offered myself, but nothing happened and I continued serving the Community and working as a Bilingual Instructional Assistant until I reached the age of 62 and I was invited to go to the yearly Itinerant's Convivence" Once there, I was sent on my first Mission: The Turks and Caicos islands in the Caribbean Sea. Seeing it as a sign from God, I responded yes to the question I was asked: Are you willing to go? And then the second question: How soon can you be ready? Two weeks after I answered, the catechist smiled and asked me to sit down. Later as the retreat was over, the team responsible for the area together with the rest of the missionary families and some single girls who were serving as teachers for the local Catholic school came to see me and welcome me very warmly. I felt happy and relieved that the waiting was over and I started to think of the things I needed to do before I go. I remember calling the responsible (a person or a family left as a contact in the Community and who organizes all the activities and events) and giving him the news. From that moment on, I was part of the itinerancy, which means that I can be sent anywhere and anytime and believe when I say that it is my experience that the Holy Spirit prepares you for that life. Every year I am invited to go to another Itinerants Convivence and I see the familiar faces of all the missionaries who are already working and also invited are the possible families and single people who might be asked to go somewhere. Most of them say yes, and that attitude helps each other to also say yes when our turn to ask comes. I've been an itinerant almost 4 years already and it's been a plentiful life, a life closer to God and to His Kingdom as I've never been or dreamed to be. One priest who has been an itinerant for many years told me that it is a privilege to be called to serve on a Mission and the freedom that you get from it, it is in itself a reward. I feel called to do this and even though it hasn't been a road of roses, it has been my daily life and I've lived it to the fullest and that is all I really need.

Philly 09/02/2015.- "The Christian is someone else." Taken from the book "Giant Surrounded by Monkeys" by Fr. Pio Carmelite. That statement implies the definition many are unaware of. A Christian is not just someone who follows Christ or becomes another Christ or Christ like, even a baptized person; no. It defines very well what it is: Someone else, someone that looks like us, eats, sleeps, walks, marries, loves, dies, etc. but it does not think like us nor reacts like us. "And I do tell you, at least you become like these children, you will not enter into the Kingdom of Heaven." Do we really understand this advice, this warning... Do we know what the Kingdom of Heaven is, how is it formed, created, who is the king of such a kingdom, who are its subjects? I asked a young man that I know, he is studying to become a seminarian (someone who is being prepared, educated to be a priest, even though the Church gives these seminarians the freedom to leave the seminary any time. The Church in its wisdom and the authority given by God, has the role to be a loving mother who admonishes and also choose those who have received the vocation to the priesthood before being ordained and, even after being ordained, these men still might change their minds and choose marriage or single lives. This person, this candidate, explained the Kingdom of Heaven compared to a place; a high and special place where there is a king and subjects of course. It may even be Heaven but he is not totally sure about the jet. He explained himself in a very childlike way:" children go near their favorite hero and want to be near him or her, surrounding them with their affection and attention. Just like Jesus want us to love Him, to wish to be with Him, put Him first in our lives, come to Him when He is near and enjoy His words, his company.``

Speaking of Heaven, the retribution of God from Heaven is being revealed against the ungodliness and injustice of human beings who in their injustice hold back the truth. For what can be known about God is perfectly plain to them, since God made it plain to them (Rm 2:4) or are you not disregarding his abundant goodness, tolerance and patience, failing to realize that this generosity of God is meant to bring you to repentance? Your stubborn refusal to repent is only storing up retribution for yourself on that Day of "retribution" when God's just verdicts will be well known. "He will repay everyone as their deeds deserve."

Philly 09/15/2015

We all come from somewhere, right? We're going somewhere. Life is a mystery too important, too precious to be just a daily routine being lived just because we have to. If that is so, why take your life? What is the hurry? How can we take it any more? Why so many babies? Schools, what is the use of so many hospitals, doctors, medicines, how come some are rich, some are poor, why do we need to have money and lots of it? There must be a good reason to live, to be born, to be here at this exactly time and society, to fall in love, to marry, travel, visit relatives, to want to have children or not to have them, to love, to have friends, to explain our situation to others, to eat 3 or 4 times a day (depending the country where we are eating, chose between drinking coffee or tea, why do the English prefer tea to any other hot drink, even though now there is Coca Cola in their country, why is the Mediterranean diet different and considered healthy, why do the Europeans drink wine? Etc… There have to be reasons for men to choose different types of food, drinks, even air lines. Why the fear of death? In our recent society, we would rather kill someone and still their organs than accept to die. Why? There has to be something marvelous, extraordinary, tremendous, extremely important that keeps us wanting to live. If that is so, let's get to it! Search, "ask and it shall be given to you" says The Lord, the Church.

Why did I marry and to such a beautiful person as Carl was, he was catholic, not that catholics are all perfect or near saints to be but I couldn't have made it a lot worse, due to my circumstances at that time.

Philly - why believe? -About and Baptism-

"In a moment, in the twinkling of an eye, as the final trumpet sounds, for the trumpet shall indeed sound, the dead shall rise incorruptible and we shall be changed." Paul's letter to the………… is indicating here that the gift of that future change will be given to those who, during their time on earth are united to Him (Jesus Christ) and his companions by upright lives within the communion of the Church. In order then, that men may obtain the transformation which is the reward of the just, (they) must first undergo here on earth a change which is God's gift. Those who in this life have been changed from evil to good are promised that future change (conversion) as a reward.

This is the secret of your formula (referring to the Neocatechumenate) which provides religious assistance, a practical training in Christian faithfulness, and effectively integrates the baptized into the community of believers which is the Church. The person who has been baptized needs to understand, to think over, to appreciate, to give assent to the inestimable treasure of the Sacrament he has received like a seed that has not yet developed.

The name Catechumenate and its intention does not invalidate or diminish the baptism currently received but the intention is to renew and practice, with time, the intensive method of the treasure of the sacrament he has received as a child.

We are happy to see that this itinerary of Faith is being received in parishes all over the world, saving separated families, baptized people far away from the mother Church, funding new seminaries where many young men are being educated and formed to become priests for the near future Church.

Pope Paul VI says: "To live and foster this re-awakening is what you call a kind of "post baptism", which can renew in our contemporary Christian communities the effects of maturity and depth which were achieved in the early church during the period of preparation before baptism. You do this afterwards. Whether before or after is secondary, I would say. The fact is that you aim at the authenticity, fullness, coherence and sincerity of Christian life."

Pope St. John Paul II says: "We (the Church) have a need of faith, of great obedience to the Church. This radicalization of faith is needed, yes, but it must always be situated within the life of the Church, and with her guidance, because the Church in her entirety has received the Holy Spirit from Christ in the persons of the apostles after His resurrection…This joy that surrounds you, that is in your songs, in your behavior, may very well be a sign of your southern temperament, but I hope it is a fruit of the Spirit. I believe that is the Spirit who initiates this way."

Philly 08/17/2015: About the Church II

O my soul. Created to enjoy such exquisite gifts, what are you doing? Where is your life going? How wretched is the blindness of Adam's children, if indeed we are blind to such a brilliant light and deaf to so insistent a voice. (From a Spiritual Canticle by st. John of the Cross) –second reading 18th week in ordinary time – Volume IV-

To be able to understand our need and rights to get to know God, the true God- it's necessary to take a journey to the past of Humanity (our own past) How life was from the beginning… and the story-our story- on the Bible. The story in the Bible starts like that: "In the beginning there was …" etc. study, learn the people's customs, how they thought, their laws, why the idols, sacrifices to their idols, their needs, why the rites (some of them we also have now) altars made with stones (the stone which the builders rejected, has become the corner stone) refers to Jesus son of the true God.

This is what, if men want to know God, the God of Abraham, Isaac and Jacob, have to read the Bible, the books that teaches about Him. Need to be close to the Word In the beginning there was the Word and the Word was God. "I am the Way, the Truth and the Life ". Men need to understand the reason for the Church (Assembly) among us, reachable and yet too far if we are not called to be part of it, a member of His body. Why the hunger, the need to feel loved, wanted by somebody. Why the search for the truth? Fear of the Lord is the beginning of wisdom. The book of Wisdom is part of the Bible together with many more, particularly the Acts of the apostles were men who are searching, looking for answers, may find the way that some church members had been following the Mission which Jesus gave them: Go and tell others even to all the nations, about me, tell them that the Kingdom of Heaven is at hand, near, even inside of us, inside of men. Those who listen and believe will be saved!. What do I need to be saved from? Come to me those we are thirsty, or hungry that I will fill you up.

Philly 09/21/2015 About Baptism and the Church

These are the teachings of one of the apostles on a letter to a community in the city of Epheso (Greece)?" Live a life worthy of the calling you have received (trough Baptism), with perfect humility, meekness, and patience, bearing with one another lovingly. Make every effort to preserve the unity which has the Spirit as its origin and peace as its binding force. (can we (humanity-society) be and live in that unity and peace without loving one another, even less say loving just our families) I would say no. Society in its whole might try to re-create such love but only up to a point, we (men) the people, could and it can be done, love a certain number of people or a certain people, for example, our children, or a teacher love the students that respond well to the rules and the teachings of the school, or we may love (not just like) those who are nice to us, but to love the enemy, the nasty one, the beggar who approaches us to beg, the robber who attacks our mother and steals her purse, oh no they are impossible to love even to forgive. To be able to do so, we need the spirit of Jesus Christ, the risen Lord, the Son of God, inside us. These are the teachings of the Church from the beginning and it always be the same. St. Paul says "I preach the cross of Christ.... (look for in the Scriptures) How do we reach that unity? The Church is one body, the body of Christ and He the head. It takes a very long time and fidelity to the Word, to the Liturgies to start to understand who this means but, its meaning is related to taking His body and His blood and by doing this –communion- we remain in His body and His body remains in us. Pure Theology is impossible to understand without the help and the teachings of the Church which as our Mother (since the Calvary) educates us and prepares us to become adult, responsible and convinced Christians.

So it is up to the faithful to build up the body of Christ, till we become one in faith and in the knowledge of God's son, and form that perfect man who is Christ come to full stature. Through him the body (the Church) grows (apostles, teaches, prophets, evangelists, pastors) and with the proper functioning of the members joined together by each supporting ligament, build itself up in love (the love of the risen Lord)

All this provides the catechumens the growth we need to remain firm in faith against the wickedness of the evil one, and in the Itinerary of faith, we are receiving this. More details about this process is explained in another chapter of the book.

Philly 08/09/2015 "I (you) am finally connected to the One I needed to be connected to, Jesus Christ the Son of God, the Head of the Church as long as I'm a member of His body'. (from the sermon of St. Augustin bishop and Doctor of the Church -33 week ordinary time second reading Wednesday "The Lord is at hand, have no anxiety" and this is the reason for our daily life activities and the culture oriented events, including the Media at all levels (film making, book publishing, news disclosure, advertising, art in general, etc.) Of course most of these had turned for the worse because it has lost the meaning based on the roots of a Judeo-Christian tradition where it has been based in the past. Society, by coming back to the mentioned values, might be able to find better, safer and logical living conditions which should take us towards a more peaceful future. (According to the reading from the treatise on forgiveness by St. Fulgentius of Ruspe, bishop 33 week Liturgy of the Hours – ordinary time) To reach this total change into perfection of the soul in its way to Heaven (Purgatory is prepared for that purpose) shall be transformed from a shameful state to a glorious one.

St. John (apostle) says: "we are now the children of God; what we shall be has not yet been revealed but we know that when it is revealed, we shall be like Him because we shall see Him as He is. (when this prophecy is fulfilled then it will be a sign.

Why believe? I asked again. About Faith. "? In a moment, in a twinkling of an eye, as the final trumpet sounds, for the trumpet shall indeed sound, the dead shall rise incorruptible and all shall be changed (Paul's letter to the Ephisians The apostle is indicating here that the gift of that future change will also be given to those who during their time on earth, are united to Him (Christ) and his companions (the Christians) by upright lives within the communion of the Church. In order then that men may obtain the transformation which is the reward of the just they must first undergo while on earth, this change which is God's gift. Those who in this life had been changed from evil to good are promised this as such reward.

Phila….08/09/2015

My visits to St. Teresa of Jesus or Teresa of Avila as we called her in some regions of Spain, have produced an extraordinary change in my soul. After the last visit I purchased the TV series and enjoyed watching it very much. I learnt so much of her personal relationship with the Lord, that invited me to begin a relationship with him too. I understood somehow that Teresa saw Jesus not only as the Lord but as a man, and as a man she treated him. Sometimes she would get angry at him and scold him almost as a wife does to a husband. Theresa is one of several Doctors of the Church and very much respected not only in Avila and Spain, but in many parts of the world. This is one of her deep thoughts: O Lord, take into account the many things we suffer on this path for lack of knowledge! The trouble is that since we do not think there is anything to know other than that we must think of You, we do not even think of You, we do not even know how to ask those who know nor do we understand what there is to ask. Terrible trials are suffered because we do not understand ourselves, and that which isn't bad at all but good we think is a serious fault. Just as cannot stop the movement of the heavens, but they proceed in rapid motion. So neither can we stop our mind. "(from the collected works of St. Teresa of Avila – volume 2 The interior Castle IV:1)

I (You) am finally connected to the one I needed to be connected to. Jesus Christ, the Son of God, the Head of the Church, as long as I'm a member of the body (the Church).

St. Augustine, bishop's sermon 33 week ordinary time 20 reading "The Lord is at (Wednesday) hand; have no anxiety"

That is the reason for life activities and the culture oriented events, the media at all levels (film making, news disclose, advertisement - advertising, etc. has turn in the worse because (as) is not based on the tradition, knowledge and education, formation of roots of a Judeo-Christian tradition, lest is way to the information and transmission of on the values (good things) by coming back (turning-towards the right direction, society will (might) be able to find a better & safer and logical living conditions and a better, peaceful future. According to the reading from the treatise on forgiveness by St. Fulgentius of Ruspe, bishop - (3 week ordinary time) Liturgy of the Hours - to reach this total change into the perfection needed to enter into heaven, (Purgatory is there for this purpose) shall be transformed from a shameful state to a glorious one.

St John says: "We are now the sons of God; what we shall be has not yet been revealed, but we know that when it is revealed we shall be like him, because we shall see him ???"

Philly, 08/20/2015

From The "Kerygma" in the shantytown with the poor- By Joseph Albiro An experience of the New Evangelization – missio ad gentes. The first community was born amongst the poor, the miserables, the unwanted. This is Joseph's experience because he packed, left everything behind his fame, friends and the comfort of his house and started sharing his life, thoughts and new feelings about God. After a profound existential crisis, an experience of conversion made him dedicate his life to Jesus Christ and to the Church. Joseph was a well known painter. In 1960, together with the sculptor Coomontes and the stained glass master Munoz De Pablos, founded the research group of Sacred Art called "Gremio 62. Joseph Albiro had exhibitions in Madrid (Biblioteca Nacional) with the group and was nominated by the Ministry of Culture to represent

Spain in the Universal Exposition of Sacred Art in Royal (France) also in 1960. He also exhibited some of his works in Holland.

Later on, Joseph meets Joy Fernandez, and, urged by the environment in which they both were living in, found a way of preaching, a kerygmatic-catechetical synthesis, that gave way to the formation of a small Christian community.

The first community was therefore born amongst the poor and rejected, in which the love of Christ crucified is made visible, becoming a "seed" that is then planted, thanks to Archbishop of Madrid, Mons. Casimiro Morcillo, in several parishes of Madrid and later in Rome and other cities in different nations. Little by little, a Way of Christian Initiation for adults begins to take shape and rediscover the riches of Baptism as its meaning as adult Christians. This Itinerary of faith helps us to renew the sacrament in all its capacity and keep us (new-catechumens) close to the Mother Church, clinging to her abundant breasts as a baby does until it receives the nourishment that it needs.

The so called the Neocatechumenal Way is now present in more than 100 nations of the five continents.. The Neocatechumenal Way is considered by now saint Pope John Paul II an "itinerary of Faith" and "of permanent education in faith". It has been recognized many times by the Church as a "gift of the Holy Spirit". Above all it is a way of evangelization for our times..

Philly 09/18/2015 Comments from St. John of the Ladder

This is what he has to say about repentance in his book "The Ladder of Divine Ascent (Greek; Klimax tou Paradise)- a classic of monastic writing- "Repentance is the renewal of baptism. Repentance is a contract with God for a second life. Repentance is constant distrust of bodily comfort. A Penitent is a buyer of humility. Repentance is reconciliation with the Lord by the practice of good deeds, mighty persecution of the stomach, and a striking of the soul into vigorous awareness."

The reality of the Christian: through sin (disobey the Commandments) we mutilate ourselves. However God has the ability to pick us up, wounded as we are, and put us back in the womb of the Church and gestate us again into a new creation.

This is The Cathecumenate's mission, before or after baptism it doesn't matter. However, the church -founders of The Way- decided to name this itinerary of faith "Neo-catechumenate" in relation with the already baptized so that the candidates would not be confused. (part of these comments taken from the book "Giant surrounded by monkeys' ' by Fr. Pius. Sammut OCD)

About my former life, I realized through the grace of God, that I have been running from my problems and sufferings since the death of my father since his present in the family was very important to me, without his support I probably was vulnerable to everything around me. I remember coming back from school and seeing his body in a coffin in the living room. I was then 11 or 12 years old and my imagination was running wild all the time. I knew that he was ill because I would see doctors coming and going from the house and one of my cousins, a nurse, was always with him in his room. My mother, busy with my little siblings, didn't pay much attention to the older ones and never mentioned to us the seriousness of the situation. After seeing his body and realizing that he was dead, my mind went out to the unknown and reality left me for some time. I think now that I reacted according to my personality and fear of death and even surprise at not experiencing sorrow. Later in live the church explained it to me. I prayed for the repose of his soul for a long time and even paid for masses as suffrage for his eternal peace. I'm at peace about myself and ready to meet him in Heaven when my turn comes. This education I'm receiving from the Catholic Church and from the Christian community where I'm being gestated according to the words that the catechists have been giving us in the name of the Lord Jesus and the inspiration of the Holy Spirit.

Philly 09/17/2015

About sacrifice: Every work that affects our union with God in a holy fellowship is a true sacrifice; every work, that is which is referred to that final end, that ultimate good, by which we are able to be in the true sense happy. As a consequence even that mercy by which aid is given to man is not a sacrifice unless it is done for the sake of God. Sacrifice, though performed or offered by man, is something divine; that is why the ancient Latins gave this name of "sacrifice", of something sacred. Man himself, consecrated in the name of God and vowed to God, is therefore a sacrifice insofar as he dies to the world in order to live for God. Works of mercy, then, done either to ourselves or to our neighbor and referred to God. This too is part of mercy, the mercy that each one has for himself. Scripture tells us: Have mercy of your soul by pleasing God.

Philly 09/16/2915

About Jesus Christ, sin, origins of life and Paradise- Christ reconciled the world with God with His own blood (do we really understand why? Why did He sacrifice his life for us? To save from what? Jesus was from the Hebrew race /his ethnicity Jewish from the house of king David all his ancestry from that nation/that people. We must know what the meaning of performing sacrifices was for them as well as the importance of their rituals, vestments and such. The building of altars of stone from the beginning of time to all gods, idols of all kinds from the time of Cain and Abel sons of Adam and Eve, our first parents according to the book of Genesis which the Jew nation have also in the Torah. God appeared to Abraham who worshiped many idols and from that moment on, Abraham built stone altars only for the new God who spoke to him and called him by his name Abram, later changed to Abraham which has a different meaning. Not only the jewish nation would build altars to Adonai, but many other peoples from other places on earth, would worship idols and built altars with burning offerings, animals and even humans were offered to their gods, later on in some countries of America, who knows for how long. Modern civilizations have found out a few centuries ago about the same tribes of native- Americans cruel ways of worship by sacrifices of children and young virgins on altars. So this method of worshiping by blood sacrifices is well known nowadays. The Catholic Mass offers a sacrifice as a way of worship accepted and shared by thousands of people all over the present world. This form of sacrifice was asked for by Jesus Christ as he celebrated the first Eucharist (Mass) with his disciples while celebrating the Passover before he was put up to death. His sacrifice on the cross was a sign of supreme love for Humanity for the remission of sins. This doctrine must be learned in the Church and understand the meaning of this act with the help of the Holy Spirit.

I would try to explain why we need to belong to the Church and remain in her as a baby attached to his/her mother, being close to her receiving the nourishment that babies need. This love was given to us when we were born in Christ and it's a love we cannot give ourselves. Once received, some little by little The Way of conversion-catechumenate, some all at once (St. Paul in his way to Damascus) it's purifying so that the Church, in the person of each of her sons and daughters, is constantly being transformed members of the "mother Church" (church meaning Assembly) gather by God Himself and the body of Christ/His Bride with Christ himself as it's head. This is the meaning of the image of the pilgrim church, a church on "pilgrimage" towards her final perfection, perfection in and by the very love that defines her in the first place. My visits to the convents renewed by St. Teresa of Avila as she is known in some regions of Spain, have produced an extraordinary change in my soul. After the last visit, I purchased the famous TV series on her life and enjoyed very much to know more about such a great saint. I learned so much of her personal relationship with the Lord that invited me to begin a relationship with Him also. Somehow I understood that Teresa saw Jesus not only as the Lord but as man, and as a man she treated Him. Sometimes she would get angry and scold Him like a wife does to a husband. Teresa is one of the several Doctors of the Church known until now and very much respected, not only in Avila and Spain but in many parts of the world. This is one of her many deep thoughts: O Lord take into account the many things we suffer on this path for lack of knowledge! The trouble is then, since we do not think there is anything to know other than we must think of You, we do not think of You, we do not even know how to ask those who know nor do we understand what there is to ask. Terrible trials are suffered because we do not understand ourselves, and that which isn't bad at all but good, we think is a serious fault. Just as we cannot stop the movement of the heavens, but they proceed in rapid motion, so neither can we stop our mind". (from the collected works of St. Teresa of Avila-Volume 2 "The interior Castle IV:1

IV CHAPTER

THE WORLD

Fresno, 10/12/1015: About Faith and Christianity -page 2

In a Christian magazine as St. Augustine once said: "A State which is not governed according to Justice (in general) would be governed by a bunch of thieves" Remota itaque iustitia quid sunt regna nisi magna latrocinia" (Latin) Fundamental to Christianity is the distinction between Church and State, meaning, as Christ himself said: "Give to Caesar what belongs to Caesar and to God what belongs to God" (Mt 22, 21) From God's standpoint, faith liberates reason from it's blind spots and therefore, helps it to be ever more fully itself. This is where Catholic social doctrine has its place, there is no intention to give/take power over the State, its aim is simply to help purify reason and to continue contributing here and now to the acceptance of the truth regarding Justice.

Christ reconciled the world with God with his own blood (according to God's plan from the beginning (do we really understand the meaning of sacrifice?) Jesus Christ was born from a Hebrew mother, the descendent of a Jewish-noble family. The story of Abraham and others tells us of this custom of offering victims as pleasing sacrifices to God, Yahveh, the Creator, the placing of stone altars in high, special places where to kill animals or people for this action. Some nations or cultures would do the same to idols pleading for favors or protection. These ceremonies were performed also by other races and religions and still now Catholics call the Eucharist the sacrifice of the Mass as Jesus comes to the altar (table) to offer himself to the Assembly in body and blood to feed us and give us his own very life with his presence.

In the Mass after being prepared in this way, Christians are sent to share the Gospel to others. This is how the Church has prepared missionaries to go to far away places or nearby places to do the work of the son of God and bring more of His creations to the knowledge of his Creator.

St. Junipero Serra, recently canonized by Pope Francis, did this by dividing his life to share his encounter with God, his faith with those who were waiting in darkness, the native-Americans. This now saint left his country, the comfort of his monastery, the love of his family and friends, to come to an unknown and dangerous place, after a perilous journey and because of a bite on the leg by an unknown animal or insect, worked miles through jungles and valleys organizing and having built the most amusing Mission-parishes imaginable. Some of these beautiful Missions, became later on important, large cities which are part of the culture and education of the State of California, a political center of this country.

Fresno, ca 10/14/2015 "Man does not look for the truth, he has to allow the truth to find him. Truth finds men. Truth is a person, Jesus Christ son of God.

(St. Augustine Doctor of the Church)

Words of pope Francis during the canonization of Fray Junipero Serra while visiting Washington D.C. on September 23th 2015. "Men know that there is something inside of us which tells us of another life, a life with meaning, a happy life and, everlasting. This invites happiness to not fill us with insatiable "placebos" . We don't want to be given the anesthesia of false ideas and live the daily routine of heartless choices.

Go and teach The Word to the others, to my brothers, says The Lord. The Church has the responsibility to speak to all the nations, and tell them what you have seen. That is the Mission of all true Christian and where they experience the joy of their call. Ir... Fray Junipero Serra. Now s saint, did it. Dedicating his entire life to serve the others, he won a place in the Kingdom. He left his land, his family, his friends, to go into an unknown and dangerous world populated by savages whose gods were constant and fierce wars against each other not knowing mercy but putting power first. Junipero departed to California full of joy, willing to die for those who considered him their enemy and with his example and unconditional love, conquered their hearts for Christ while living behind the faith of the Church that had sent him in the name of Jesus. The Missions that he and his companions founded along the California coast, all named after important saints, are still being used as living and popular communities, for the glory of God in the name of the history of California and

Fresno, 10/12/2015: Our Lady of Pilar ``Patroness of the Hispano-America. God is not real, why the deep desire to be good and do things well. I've read that some philosophers said that "If God does not exist, we'd have to invent it" Which is what leads some nations to think that the Church (The Vatican, the popes, priests, etc. had done. Marxism believes says that "the poor do not need charity but justice!" I must ask Where does Justice begin? Where does it come from? Where're its limits and the steps, the rules to reach it? How many decisions to make to be just? All these questions and more are in the back of my mind and of the minds of many. Only Christians seem to have the answers. The visit of the Pope to Philadelphia during September of 2015 moved thousands of families from around the world to hear his message, to enjoy his presence and his company. His goal was to share the message of love and unity which begins in and by the family. This very important message can only be completed in and within families, Christian families or families who are preparing to be Christians. What is a Christian?. A Christian is another Christ, a perfect image-reproduction of the son of God.

GOD CALLS ME BY MY NAME

The day came when we had to fly from Fresno to London, so we went. The boys, my companion and I. The plain we took from Fresno was small, perhaps 8 to 12 seats maybe more and my sons were excited but a little scared as they new that something was wrong, fortunately they were too young to understand and went along with me We, my children and I, have always had good communication and I believed they trusted me. We flew from Fresno to Los Angeles. Angeles and non-stop to London. Once we got there, everything went easter, my sister picked us up and went to her home in the London's suburbs. The children had been playing with some other kids on the plain and somehow got a virus that kept them in bed for several days. They were happy to be with their aunt and cousins. The next day my sister called her family doctor and he cared for the boys until they were well and we then took off for Madrid. I was excited to be in my country again and of course with my family even though they did not agreed with my decision and some of my relatives gave me a piece of their minds, all of then helped us and welcomed us with open arms but they had their fears about if I had made the right choice by running away like that, secretly and hiding from my husband like if he were some kind of lunatic, crazy man. Little had they known that that was exactly how I saw him every time that he was drank. I was separated from my husband for three years, legally divorced for one and all that time looking for true love on the account of my father's lost affection and the emptiness of my longing for his presence. Time went by fast while I looked for work, took care of my brother's house, partied with his friends and wasted my life looking for love in "all the wrong places" like an old country hit said. I had multiple sexual partners most of them young lonely men looking for adventure in the darkness of the night, trying to find a good time which would helped them to forget their boring lives also without love; their lives being just a series of empty days one after the other. I would work here and there to contribute to the expenses of the family, my brother and his alcoholic wife. They had three children then even though, after my brother started going to Church, they had two more. One of the jobs I had was an English teacher, the The condition to get it was that I had to be an American because everybody in Spain then wanted to learn from a native teacher so I lied and I got the job. I would go to work and leave my son Michael with some of the homeless people whom my brother would let in from the street. Thank God that nothing happened to him and nobody hurt him in any way or so I thought. Anyhow he never told me of anything harmful happening to him while I was away and that is another great miracle.

Now I can say that I've been taking care of myself for a long time now because, according to the Scriptures "You are to love others as yourself" , that if you don't love yourself and care for yourself, you would be unable to love. Again the law made for us can go against us and judge us. Life is limited, because God gives time to us to make the best of it, to answer to His calling and find Him. Life make seem long sometimes but it is not but very short, compared to eternity and if we find or when we find the way to the "good life" then we can live our life as we are supposed to do which is doing good, serve the others, find LOVE to give it and to enjoy it. Life is a very serious matter but many times, some of us or perhaps many of us try to find our own happiness Adam's way: "The woman that You gave me, made me eat" and that is the core of the first fall, blame the other for my actions, don't worry, be happy, ='Acuna Matata' etc. Faith is a virtue and it is given to us by God Himself and the Administrator is the Church and faith is about believing in God and not only in Him but in everything that comes from Him and His son came from Him for a Mission, to give himself as the price that (humanity) we're supposed to pay instead. Once we are rescued, we need to acknowledge this action and see ourselves being rescued. A process of a spiritual nature which has to be initiated by the Holy Spirit Himself. I've always been looking for "truth" and that search took me to maybe the scientific truth or the truth in nature or the generic type of truth but not to the real truth. When Jesus talks to Pilate the governor of Judea at the time of his death, He has a short conversation with him and tells him that He has been born for this, to bear witness to the truth and all who are on the side of truth listen to my voice" then Pilate says: Truth? What is that? So, there is a truth and some of us or maybe all of us at different moments in our lives would look for it but, we has to be enlighten to recognize it when we hear it and that is what happened to me: I was ready to listen because I had suffered and struggle and was wounded and needed help. I'm trying very hard to explain myself and my situation at the time that I found the "truth" that Jesus was talking to Pilate about. Only through Jesus we can accept suffering, any kind of suffering and by receiving His Spirit we become like Him (Christians) being the new creation that The Bible is talking about: the New Adam, the new man able to love in the (dimension of the cross) and to understand the sufferings and tribulations that come with life which are part of everybody's life.

I was 17 when president John F. Kennedy was assassinated. On that sad day I was in Madrid, Spain getting ready to go to work. We didn't own a TV set yet and the radio was on. My mother was in bed in her bedroom when I heard the spokesman say that the president of the USA has been shot in Dallas, Texas as the car where he and his wife Jackie were saluting the Texan population who was standing and greeting him back along the sidewalk down the avenue towards their destination. A tragic visit where death was waiting behind a dusty small window situated on the top floor of an old building across from where the presidential car was to pass. I didn't know then that some years later, I would be standing exactly at the same spot where the shooting took place. During the years 2007 to 2009 I was sent to work in a parish in the small town of Grand Prairie situated 25 miles from Dallas. Texas is the home state of my husband. His family were born in the south near the Mexican border at the Rio Grande valley and actually most of them are still living there, some had moved towards the north. One of his aunts lives in Corpus Christi, others in Weslaco which is the small town where my husband was born. The valley is a very rich land with many trees and fields where some of the best grapefruits in the world are grown there, together with other types of citrus and plants. Agriculture is most popular in that area since the soil is best near the great river which crosses the south valley towards the Mexican border. I've learnt all this when I lived there and I was delighted to have been given the opportunity to know the land that my husband was so proud of. He was a real Texan tall and strong and a real Dallas fan (the famous football team) . I enjoy the time that I lived there and I always try to know more of the history of this gigantic and great state. I still have many friends there and I kept contact with some of the members of my husband's family who were glad that I was so close by and willing to get in touch with them. The church in Texas is being renewed through the Neo- catechumenal Way and God is sending many missionaries both single and families who are giving their lives to spread the Gospel and to be present as the Domestic Church as the Catechists called it because this brothers and sisters are really giving the sign of love and unity which is what Community is made of. The Gospel is preached without ceasing and the Holy Spirit is flowing around all over with its powerful presence of Love among those who carry it with them. I am very happy to have been part of this wonderful reality seeing how the Word of God (Jesus Christ) is being sown in every corner of the world as it has been promised by The Lord Himself in the Holy Scriptures and through the people whom has been chosen to do this important and necessary Mission: to spread the Good News everywhere that it is needed. Christ needs to be announced by The Church before the end of the times as it is written it has to be done. It is a duty done gladly by the Christians because of this news and that Spirit it is not for us, but to share it with others. I am seeing the "occupy" at Manhattan NY and I can't help but think that there is no human reason to be doing that "so called occupation" on ??? or any other area of any city in any country, those demonstrations are totally useless out of touch. This country and others are in a state of financial crisis produced by many facts and situations which have been handed down to this generation at this particular moment and it is nobody's fault. I see the faces of the "demonstrators' ' showing rage and bitterness and I can't help but feel sorry for them. People blaming Eve again, Eve blaming Adam and history begins. Paradise is not situated on earth but it is a place outside of our present human reality. Blaming the finance's gurus and executives who are doing their jobs the best that they can, it's not going to solve our situation. On the contrary, they are doing the money exchange games which have been putting money in the pockets of millions of people who play these games and are free to do so. When I see the ignorance of this generation I tremble and feel that we are wrong once more and violence would not answer our questions of any kind. I can't stop saying the same thing over and over again. Jesus is the one, He is the new man, He can show us the way to happiness beyond our wildest dream. I receive what I need according to my needs and as Sta. Teresa of Avila says: 'Solo Dios basta" (Only God satisfies)

III CHAPTER
JUICE, COFFEE, TEA

It's 9:07 PM Halloween 2011. The 3 Mission Girls (that is how missionary women are called in the Neo-cat itinerary) and I am one of them, have moved from Central Avenue to 10th street close to the Mission family who lived down the street from us. Also next door lives a lady who works at St. Anthony of Padua parish as a volunteer.

She helps with the administration and the church parking which is rented on a daily basis to people who come to work in the area and, because of their work, can't be controlling the time of expiration in the parking meters located everywhere in the streets of Union City. So I am here enjoying the new place. It is a nice, clear, old wooden floor apartment with many windows and a blue bathtub which reminds me of the ocean when I'm taking a bath in it. The night is quiet and I don't see many children trick-and-treating at this hour and I'm thinking that perhaps they're already savoring the candy and treats at home. This year the weather has been different and unexpected. Just to give you an example, yesterday Sunday it snowed for hours until it reached over 10 inches of white, soft and floating flakes of the thickest snow fall I've ever seen. I heard on the radio that New Jersey hasn't seen snow so early in the year and so heavy since the 1920's; so many homes are still without electricity and probably frizzing and waiting for the electric Company to repair the damages caused by the storm while celebrating this complex evening which comes all the way from the early ages of Civilization and the Christian Culture. The festivity of All the Saints is tomorrow November the 1st and the evening of that special day is like a vigil commemorating the lives and holy souls of the saints who have preceding us to Heaven because they had served God with all their minds, their might and their hearts accomplishing the Shema which is the Jewish tradition of keeping God in their lives and honoring Him at all times and offering all they have. I learnt that this tradition was taken and misstep into the popular Halloween or Holy evening being interpreted in a different light and for a different reason, of course later on it has been commercialized and turned into a profit day where candy is used and consumed in enormous quantities and sizes. I'm listening to an interesting radio station where it's host Delila has been charming with her friendly greetings to all the people trick-and- treating "out there" while she chats with the night callers one at a time who ask for special tunes to dedicate them to their special someone. So, at this quiet hour I am thanking God for all His blessings and tender mercies to me and I am ending this day and still going along with it and thinking of all the things that He has allowed me to do, create and perform to the best of my knowledge which He has put in me anyway and because of His grace, gifts and talents I can serve in the Mission I've been given until He decides to use me for something else or ends the life that He created for me with ups and downs, hills and valleys and everything else which comes with the package. I pray in silence during this time at night to send me angels to guide me to Him.

My Life 12-17-2011

As I was trying to explain on my previous page, "the new man, the new Adam, as being made in the likeness of sinful humanity, had taken on himself the nature of our first parents (Adam and Eve) unless he had stooped to be one in substance with his mother while sharing the Father's substance mand, being alone free from sin, united our nature to his, the whole human race would still be held captive under the dominion of Satan. The Conqueror's victory would have profited us nothing if the battle had been fought outside our human condition. But through this wonderful blending the mystery of new birth shone upon us, so that through the same Spirit by whom Christ was conceived and brought forth we too might be born again in a spiritual birth; and in consequence the evangelist declares the faithful to have been born not of blood, nor of the desire of the flesh, nor of the will of man, but of God." These are the precise words taken from a letter by Saint Leo the Great, pope, and only a great man like him could put the mystery of the incarnation of the new man into Humanity to become one like us "in everything except in sin" as the scripture says. And I say, a society immersed in the discovery of new cells, and new worlds and new ways to take us a step farther into perfection, is it so blind to the true and better nature who comes from above, to put it plainly from beyond our planet earth as we know it? this is one of the questions floating in my mind most of the time until I read the words taken from the Bible and I find the answer to most of them. All my life I've been listening to stories from people who had seen "ovnis", "Ufos" or whatever we wish to call them. Hundreds of books, fiction or not fiction about people from another planet, aliens and such, invaders from other worlds, without forgetting all the information from Hollywood with all their ideas on the subject and even people who had joined different Clubs where they investigate together and exchange experiences and information about it. Why on this day and age of out of space encounters and knowledge, I say why is it so hard to understand and believe the story of one who came from "another place" to live among us, a real "superhero" who survived his own death to prove to us (everyone) that death has been submitted and subjected to Him who conquered it and that there is a God, a superior Being who created everything that we can see and cannot see, every planet, every star, every animal, water, the oceans, separated land from sea, made the heavens and the rivers and then created a human being into His image and likeness so that someone could enjoy creation and share the life with God's life and then after his human body reaches its end, the end of the flesh as we know it, mankind may continue living for ever because not only there might be life in other planets but to know that there is life in another place and that place is called Eternal Life or Heaven, a place of happyness beyond our human capacity of understanding and assimilation. But only through the Mother Church we can enter into this divine revelation which resides in The Word and the Church is the administrator and custodian of this knowledge which everyone can reach regardless of his/or her situation as long as we say yes to His invitation to believe and accept His son Jesus as the one who came to saves us and rescued us from dying the "other death" the situation that the Church calls Hell. I've been in Hell as the prayer The Creed says and while I was there in my sins and in my misery and blindness, Jesus descended into hell and rescued me and brought me up, lifted me up to a level which was solid enough for me to put my feet on it and get my head out of the mire of quicksand which was my life then.

Mother's Day finds me in my apartment. It is sunny and nice and I feel good because my son Michael, the priest, has called me to wish me a Happy Mother's Day. I am waiting to be picked up to go to the house of a couple from my community which had invited me to eat with them and spend some of the feast accompanied. It is a good idea since I expected to spend the day by myself. Thank God that I am available for these types of invitations and willing to have them. It is very different living in a Christian Community in Church…life goes on enriching you and taking you farther on one step at a time. Once I was explaining to a priest how I am walking The Way (an Itinerary of conversion to Faith) and he didn't understand, and if a priest doesn't understand I can't think of all others (whom) are not guided by the Holy Spirit. What I've told him was that time moves in an eternal way. Catechists called it another dimension. "to enter into the dimension of the Cross" and that is what it feels like. Of course, to understand this concept you need to be walking on it and going towards Heaven and following The Lord, then this new Way begins to make sense. So now that my son called me, Mother's Day is fulfilled for me and now, after this day is almost over, I think that I had a very special day. A family from my community invited me over to their home to enjoy a barbecue accompanied by one of the family children's birthdays. The outing was a total success and we all had a very happy time. My extended family, as some people called the Church community, really did it's Mission and the hospitality that I've received made everything perfect. The first time I heard the Greek word "Agape" or "Charity Love, I didn't know what it meant until the team who was given the Catequesis explained the meaning to us; then I understood. The New Testament uses it several times and St Paul explains it and uses it often enough to understand. It is a New Kind of Love, he says and he also says that at the time of the Romans and because of the culture then, it was necessary to explain it in different ways. Before Jesus came to the world to fulfill his Mission, the world understood the word Love in many ways, always related it to human love, physical love, passionate love, as we know it but, as the Church starting forming and moving forward it wasimportant to make another meaning to the word Love. It is because of this that the word Agape=Charity or brotherly Love, was invented by the first Christians and it has been used even since in Church and Society.

My life (a lesson from church (according to the Vatican II Council, 1965)

From the pastoral constitution on the Church in the modern world of the II Vatican Council (Gaudium et spes, nn. 37-38) "Holy Scriptures, with which the experience of the Ages is in agreement, teaches the human family that human progress, though it is a great Blessing for man, brings with it a great temptation. When the scale of values is disturbed and evil becomes mixed with good, individuals and groups consider only their own interests, not those of others. The result is that the world is not yet a home of true brotherhood, while the increased power of mankind already threatens to destroy the human race itself. If it is asked how this unhappy state of affairs can be set right, Christians state their belief that all human activity, in daily jeopardy through pride and inordinate self-love, is to find its purification and its perfection in the cross and resurrection of Christ."

I was in "the world" and now I'm in the Church and it is a fact not a thought because there is a world (God created it) and there is the Church, a church because Jesus Christ founded just one and how did He founded it? By sending the disciples first two by two when He was still with them, in the flesh, and then, after He was killed in front of everybody up on a hill so that He could be seen, starting appearing to different people (Scriptures said that He appeared to more than 500 people all of them at the same time) right after His crucifixion and while all the 11 disciples, remember than Judas was no longer with them because he had hanged himself from a tree outside the Jerusalem wall, anyhow His mother Mary was also in the company of the disciples as John, the disciple that Jesus specially loved, has accepted her as his own mother and took her home to live with him, according to the Scriptures Jesus proclaimed His mother Mary the mother off all nations and peoples and John understood that as his mother she should come to live with him and so he did. For now, everything makes perfect logical sense, no? it is a very human request since she was already a widow and now after his death, she would also be alone. But I was trying to explain how the Church came about and it was something that started little by little by the preaching of the news of these men and also a few women who have been witnesses to a extraordinary event, and how these "scare cats" could have the courage to go out and shout to everybody they saw on the streets, that the man than they have kill (remember that the groups reunited outside the roman court's patio asked for the release of Barabbas and the death of Jesus) was really the Messiah and that they had receive His resurrected spirit and the Mission to "go and announce to their brothers that the Kingdom of Heaven was at hand" So that the people who would listen seriously and believed the message would become "believers" or "followers" of this dead Jesus whom they've accepted as the Messiah promised by God and announced through the prophets. These listeners would probably approached the disciples after they had done the announcement and asked them (as John the Baptist's disciples asked him) "Now what do we have to do?" (*) and received instructions to continue meeting and to wait for more information or perhaps the disciples would impose their hands over their heads and they would receive the Holy Spirit or something like that. I'm speaking with the knowledge that I have of how the Church is being rebuilt and renewed now since the beginning of the Vatican II Council and the reforms and changes which came from its actions and solutions. These insights and others inspired by the preaching of the Catequesis had inspired me to get to these and other conclusions of how the Church, as we know it, was formed. So the Church is not a building or an Organization but a body of people (rearming and representing the Body of Christ) who move around sharing the news with other people who might or might not be expecting to receive them. I still don't know exactly how but the fact is that I received the News, accepted it, somehow believed (inspired by the Holy Spirit) and started walking towards

The Light and away from the darkness where I had fallen without even realizing it and then it all began…..

I didn't wanted this day to end without writing a few lines and commenting that tonight another missionary woman, the wife of the family mission that came to joint St. Anthony's a few weeks ago and I had done "traduccion" which is announcing the Good News to the parishioners of the area by sharing our experience of the Love of God in our lives. This custom (which it's been in the Church from its beginnings) and The Way is recuperating as so many more customs and traditions. We visited some of the houses and greeted the families and, if they let us in and are willing to listen, we go in and talk. I received more than I gave and sharing what God has done in my life always helps me to remember and be grateful, specially now being so close to Thanksgiving. After the visits, we went back to the Parish of St. Anthony's for Mass and I prayed for the soul of my mother because today is the feast of St. Elizabeth of Hungary her name saint day. All together a memorable ending to a very good day and my heart goes up full of gratitude to God for giving us such a nice day. When listening to my traduccio partner my mind was floating towards how my life was before I received the News of Salvation. Because "you cannot believed if you don't see a Christian" my catechists use to say all the time, and it is true and I had seen many Christian in Church giving their lives and time to spread the Gospel and loving when there is no human reason to love, till the end of every day, attentive to everybody's needs and pains, listening to our problems and complaints and loving us all the way. These brothers and sisters stay with you from the beginning of your walk till the end and many of them burry us and accompany us our place of rest. They accompanied us when my husband passed away, helped us to prepare the funeral and all the ceremonies and sustained us (my sons and I) in our hour of weakness and sadness even though I was not sad beyond reason because I know that Heavens exists and tonight during the sharing of our encounter with God, I heard it over and over again as my partners experience was about that, God has put in her heart that Heaven is a fact, and she is certain of it and speaks of it with such convincement that it touched my heart once and again and the visits enriched my evening more that I expected and I receive in giving the greeting of Peace to everyone who opened the door to us, a peace that only Jesus can give as He explained and gave it to His disciples after His resurrection. The peace that "is not of this world" according to His words and, as I remember the news of the day and those persons who are complaining and protesting because they don't have what it was suppose to come to them and they are angry and frustrated and don't want to wait anymore and at the end nobody really knows what they want and why are these people making such a fuss about being poor and not having a job and so forth because it is nobody's fault really and nobody can fix their problem and make their 'dream" come true because they are not dreaming anymore but awake because the cruel reality has come to their lives and they were not prepare to accept it. The Wall Street protesters are a sad sight for all Americans and the rest of the world wonders what has gone wrong with the American Dream but, what they don't know is that the protesters are not dreaming anymore but are demanding a future which they didn't build themselves. May God help them to understand and also help us to understand them and not to judge their unclear motives to get attention and upon all love.

  The life that The Lord has allowed me to live until now it's been the rock on which my actual life can be lived and without the past, there will be no future and because Life is Eternal, the future is endless, there to be lived. I do not know if I'm making any sense but it is my experience and the words that I write are part of me. It is what I am today as the way has been open in front of me to follow. The story has been written already and all I have to do is walk, fill the voids and do my part. As I was talking in the previous chapter about the pilgrimage to Denver with my family, memories started to move in my mind and other trips with its own experience came to me with sheer clarity. Israel, Canada, France, Germany, Australia have been points of enlightening and spiritual awakening for me and I know that I've been chosen to receive such gifts and to add those wonderful events to my life. Perhaps I should add that in an empty vessel like me, to be filled with such graces represents an immense accomplishment and my soul "rejoices" as Mary the Blessed Mother of God said in the lively song Magnificat, in God my (Salvador) who has put His eyes on me and pull me out of the pit of death to make with in a story of salvation not only for myself but for the rest of my family, relatives, friends, (vecinos) co-workers, and every person who might come in contact with me and my new life. All those encounters with my fellow Catholics, the closeness of the mother Church with its Head, the Pope representing the Son of God the Head of the Body, The Universal Church. The youth screaming with joy to be in the presence of the figure of Peter the Rock listening to his encouraging words, words of eternal life and beautiful promises of eternity, of a Love which never ends and that Life has a meaning which is to love the other as yourself and the Church gives us the Holy Spirit so that we can fulfill this (mandamiento) and live a happy, holy life however difficult it would be holy because it is His will being done and not ours with the usual ups and downs, despairs and errors that make us chose the wrong solutions to problems which are there to help us mature and give us the knowledge that we need to live the "good life" The life of Grace being purified by the Church on a daily basis, and infused in our souls through the Sacrament of Baptism, would take us to become the person who God intended when He created us and in this way we come to please Him as Jesus pleased Him because as parts of His Body and heirs of the Kingdom we are His children too. It is my hope that all these encounters and personal experiences had made on me a difference and the blessings and graces which I've receive from them, would act in my soul as the vaccination against the attacks of the devil who is waiting to make me sin and to make me doubt of the Love of God for me because even though all these signs of Faith and confirmation of His intervention in my life and of the lives of my family are very strong, the world and the flesh can be stronger and the lies of the evil one can damage the life of grace. Mercy Lord for we are weak.

I have been a pilgrim all my life but I didn't know. The Church teaches that all Christians are pilgrims because we are passing by in this life to go to the real life which (is) Eternal. It's not easy to accept and less yet to understand. We are all born with a seed of eternity and most of our lives we spend sleeping and dreaming and, even though when we are physically awake, we are not all there in our reality, therefore we start to live as we are touched by God Himself through Jesus Christ of course!. Speaking of being a pilgrim, I've been one and experienced it completely several times because by the grace of God I went to the World Youth Day which was celebrated in Denver, Colorado in 1993. We went together as a family and also as part of our Church Community, we saw other pilgrims, hundreds of them, shared with them the happiness of the Church united in the same spirit, while waiting for the vicar of Peter the first Pope. I remember that some of the members of the first community took a small group of teens and one adult, a single man who was somehow out of place and looking for meaning for his life, perhaps even a vocation. We crossed California to Phoenix, spent some time with the small communities of that city and continued north towards Denver. We and another family drove two minivans through the beautiful Colorado desert and I enjoyed both the view from the minivan window and the joy of the young members of the community who were having a great time on this trip. Their humor was contagious and we all had a good time. Once in Denver, we visited different religious places, prayed, read our personal Bibles on the bus and enjoyed each other's company and experiences of faith. There were some priests accompanying us and also teams of catechists who helped to organize the Pilgrimage. We had cantors with their guitars, married couples being assigned as chaperons. The buses stopped at designated points, we visited splendorous Catholic Sanctuaries and parishes to celebrate the Eucharist and many more interesting things. All together a most memorable Journey but the best part was to receive the pope Blessed John Paul II and to be with him listening to his wise words, seeing the love he shared with all of us and specially the young people who had a closed encounter with him, almost like a father and child relationship, something special that I can't describe. This event touched our hearts and for my husband and myself was a seal which the Church put on our marriage, the promise that God's grace would be with us because He made possible our reconciliation and because of it, we were present there as part of the Universal Church, members of the Body of Christ. One of the days we were there, some of us were dancing and singing on the streets of Denver when all of a sudden, a ring of soft colors started to form in the sky above us like a message from Heaven telling us that there was gladness because we were singing, dancing and celebrating as the pilgrim Church who has come to gather and welcome the Vicar of Christ on Earth. Both our sons received a vocation for life. Christopher to the marriage life (his girlfriend has come with us) and Michael John the vocation to the priesthood. My husband and I were pleased and thankful for it. Two years later he passed away peacefully because he knew that God has His hand on them and that I will not be alone. I am just that we went.

When my husband and I went to talk to the bishop of Fresno about having the Communities and the Neo-catechumen ate (itinerary of Faith) restarting in our parish St. John's Cathedral. It was the end of summer 1987, my husband and I were sitting outside in the backyard having a cool bear both dressed in shorts for the heat at the beginning of the evening and the phone rang. I don't remember who answered but who called: our good friend and pastor Rev Pat McCormick and he gave us the best news we have had in a very long time. You see, I needed my little Christian community which my sons and I left to come back home because even though I was happy that I was back and I knew and experienced everyday that God was putting our lives together day by day, I still needed to listed to The Word, to joint the Assembly (the Church) and to walk the Tripod (the Way goes supported on the three legs: The Word, The Liturgy and The Community) and I knew what I was missing and even though my husband Carl was satisfied and happy that we had returned, his need for The Church wasn't the same as mine. He hasn't been called yet to joint the communion of Saints and his idea of going to Church was to dress up on Sunday morning and go to

Mass, as the majority of the Catholics do and I understood him and didn't blame him because I knew that his time was coming. We ran to the car and to the Cathedral and were taken upstairs to a small private sitting room where we talked with both the Pastor and the Vicar who was a very nice priest who had come to the US as a refugee from Cuba. The date was set to start the Catequesis and we went back home happy and excited for the news. I was to walk again and be a part of a Christian Community!!! God hasn't forgotten about us and His plan was full ahead. The time came for the Catequesis to begin and we announced it everywhere even at the Sunday Masses. Fr. Sancho was happy and hopeful and he prepared the way for the team of Catechists coming from L.A. to give the chats. When the time came, the small community was formed and a group of people of all ages and conditions started the special walk towards adult Faith. To my despair, after only a few weeks of walking, the Community separated into small groups and we didn't see it again. I was heartbroken and sad and the only thing that would make it better was the daily Mass and that's what I did, go to Mass everyday and pray for the chance to have another Catequesis. In 1989 we went to Spain on vacation and to visit the family. That year the World Youth Day was to be at Santiago de Compostela in the northeast part of Spain, Galicia and to my surprise, our oldest son was invited and he went with some of his cousins to participate and celebrate. When he came back, he was enlightened, extremely happy and excited and we rejoiced with him and his experience. I know that he has seen God and I felt relieved. Back in the States, I was inspired by the Holy Spirit to go to talk to the Bishop of Fresno and ask him to allow the

Catequesis in the Diocesis and to give us permission to walk again. I cried like a baby and touched the Bishop's heart. My husband accompanied me and he was a great support for me. He cooperated, collaborated and exposed himself to the Bishop with all his heart. We'd told him about our reconciliation after almost being divorced for 4 years and showed him photos of celebrations that I had previously joined the Community which was formed at The Cathedral. He liked what he heard and treated us with great concern and tenderness and after a while and much begging in our in part, he gave his consent to us having Catequesis and funding small Christian Communities the way it was planned to be from the beginning. When we went home I was very pleased and thanked the Lord for His Mercy and also started to prepare for the next step.

9/11 2011 was a beautiful day!! Our church community (the 3rd of Holy Redeemer Parish west New York) had our monthly retreat - Convivencia- and we had a wonderful one. All the brothers and sisters pray Lauds (the morning prayer of the Church) together, we sang together with the children, bless the children after the first part of the prayer, send them out to play with the babysitter and continued, only the adults, until Lauds was over, it must have been around 12:30 pm and after the kiss of peace ritual we went to the dining room to have lunch. The food was rich and abundant and we had a very pleasant time. One of the brothers brought a bottle of rich, red wine and the conversation was cheerful and relaxing. After lunch, some of the sisters stayed behind to clean the dining room and picked up and rejoined the rest of the assembly to continue to share our experiences of the month and the summer in general, after which we finished with the retreat, greeted each other and went home. Because we had been expecting a Mission family to join the evangelization process at the Parish of St. Anthony of Padua, the pastor, Fr. Jose called me to ask me if I could organize a light supper for the family who is coming from Spain this evening. The idea was to give them a nice warm welcome, something to eat and take them to their new place, a nice 2 bedroom by the parish. This family is from Valencia, have two children, both boys and are very much needed to help to do many things. The brothers and sisters who are walking at St. Anthony's has been helping to provide furniture and household goods for their apartment and everybody is very excited and happy to have the opportunity to welcome them. Last night during the Eucharist which was celebrated at Manhattan, New York the people talked about the memories at Ground Zero and prayed for the dead and for their families and altogether it was a memorable event. A son of one of the firemen who gave his life trying to save others was also present at the Mass and some of the pilgrims returning from the World Youth Day at Madrid, Spain shared their experience at this special gathering. While they were talking I imagined a tired but smiling Pope who gave his time and energy to meet with almost 2 million young people coming from all parts of the world. To me the event confirms the faith of Peter among the next generation so needed by the Catholic Church at this difficult moment when the Catholic church is under much attack and persecution even though it is happening slowly and in a very "civilized" way. I know that to me and many people, this gathering represents Jesus and the Church being called to receive the same spirit and to a life of service and adult faith much needed and searched by everybody looking for the true answer to the difficult times which we are experiencing at the present. To be able to experience this witnessing of young people moving unstoppable to spend a few days with each other as The Universal Church and it's head Pope Benedict XVI is an out of this world experience, a renewal of the seed planted in us through baptism and a tremendous call to life when the world is submerge into a deep whole of despair only compared to be waiting at the Gates of Hell knocking at nothing while at the same time expecting a faint call for help which is trapped down into the souls of all of us.

THE PERSON WHOM I WAS AND HOW I USED TO THINK

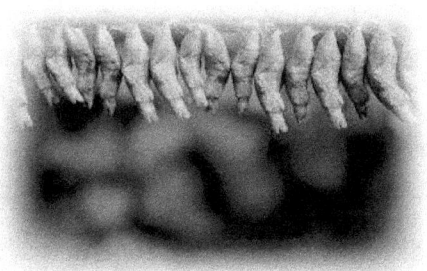 

The unhappy times which I've lived, I cannot get back and, according to the teachings of Mother Church, I will always carry it with me in my soul and my new glorious body. There is so much that I need to learn, so much that I must believe, so much I need to forgive. All the times that I've been rude, selfish. Every time that I hurt someone, every time that I lied, every time that I've deceived anyone, made fun of anyone, hated anybody When I've been thinking only of me, taking care of me, all the times that I planned against my husband, my mother, my sisters, my friends. Every time that I judged them, despised them, rejected them, ignored them, not listening to, every time that I thought only of myself and my satisfaction I have sinned. And we don't understand sin, the Media makes fun of it, society ignores it but every sin counts and it must be redeemed, declared and forgiven. I didn't understand sin until I was invited to a Penance Celebration which is a Liturgy of the Word accompanied by the Sacrament of Penance- what it was called Confession. This celebration is part of the catequesis or chats which exposed Jesus Christ to the people who gather to listen to the 'Good News" (this is the meaning of the word Gospel). After receiving the Sacrament and after I've confessed my recent sins, which were very clear to me since my adulteries were well known by every member of my family, plus all the men that I have been committed adultery with, I went into a state of what the Church calls Grace and remembering my past life and all the hurt that I've caused I felt warm tears falling from my eyes. At the same time, a feeling of repentance was so strong that I had to leave the assembly and waited outside. The aridity of my heart had turned into a profuse desire for change and for the first time of my life I understood the words" conversion" and "repentance". Someone came out to see how I was doing, I don't remember who but this person counseled me and helped me to understand my feelings and the sorrow that I was experiencing. From that day on, the Future opened for me, a heavy burden was removed from my shoulders and the joy of freedom started to move inside me with great force. My relations starting to change, my actions made sense, my entrails began to love my sons with a tenderness which I've never felt before. My sons would come with me to church and they knew that something supernatural had taken place, and accepted it well even though I couldn't explain everything that was happening to me. Immediately after a Community was formed, my oldest son Christopher, started to be prepared for First Communion and I was filled with an enormous sense of responsibility for his spiritual welfare. My church community cooperated in all aspects of the event, helped me to prepare my son for this important time of his life and the time came when he received communion for the first time. I believed that he was proud and happy on that special day. I know I was.

It is a very quiet Sunday indeed everything "all is quiet in the Western Front", as an old movie classic will say. The sun shines fiercely and summer is in full bloom once more, making everything slow and shade searching like we used to do as kids. I look around and I see plenty of fresh water ponds, horses drinking and grazing in a comfortable way not treating but gently. These beautiful animals make me want to go near them to ride them; I will if I only knew how! It is a fun thought and I enjoy thinking about it because I've always been attracted to horses though I've never been close to them long enough to get familiar with their presence around me. Now at my age, I regret not being able to enjoy them. The narrow road which runs parallel to the rails looks empty and dry and I feel happy that I'm on the train, cool and protected. The train is starting to go down into the valley, the small hills slowly getting behind and the splendor of the fruit trees take their place in the scenery. Gently, the leaves on the new corn bend under the sun which gives them a golden touch. This is farm country now and they appear here and there showing how important they are for the people, providing food, cattle and grain at the right time. I can't help thinking of the efforts of farmers and their dedication to the soil so rich and ready that it made them proud. Food is the most precious resource we receive from The Creator…not to forget His bounty and love. I looked up and saw the clouds white like soft big cotton balls showing at the distance making the scene perfectly complete. The train stops at a station and I'm glad that it is not my stop because it is late in the afternoon, the heat is rising and I'm not looking forward to leaving the cool hospitality of the Amtrak train. This trip is one of the many trips that I took by train since my husband passed away. I try to remain active, visit friends and relatives as we used to do when we were together. Feed my brain so I would not get Alzaimers and use my time the best way I knew how. I would love to sit by the window to look at the scenery and sometimes get a piece of paper and try to describe what I saw, even a napkin from the café-car will do. Time will go faster and I really have fun doing it. Putting on a paper what I saw and felt while looking is not easy but the words come to me Through my eyes and In my mind I would find hundreds of words trying to come out to describe as accurately as possible whatever I was looking at. Since Spanish is my mother language, sometimes I would be thinking in Spanish and writing in English and that is not a simple task. So the process was entertaining and exciting and it was good training for my brain.

If I wouldn't have a Word Processor in my computer, I don't think I would write, but I do make it easier. The years after our Reconciliation were good, better than good,. We took walks, had conversations, made love, laughed and looked at each other like we had just met. During those first days, we visited some of the Missions of California with our sons, went to the beach, went shopping, watched TV together and visited some of our friends and relatives who we hadn't seen for quite some time. Ray will make breakfast and read the newspaper while I take the boys to school. Sometimes, he'll get drunk and we will have terrible fights and he will smack me around a little bit. My son Michael would try to stop us and he would also be pushed out of the way. Our older son was too hurt to get involved and maybe a little ashamed, instead he would stay in his room until it was over. I am very thankful that we decided to talk to our Pastor about our problem as we offered him The Way and gave him our experience of reconciliation and God's intervention to bring us to it, because he advised us to see a marriage counselor and we went. A few sessions by ourselves and then with our sons all together as a family. The experience was educational and effective and we would talk about our unresolved issues and all the wrong choices that were made because we were a dysfunctional family dependent on alcohol to relate with each other. Just the discovery of the illness and its influence on all the areas of our lives, was extremely enlightening and because the counselor was catholic working for the catholic church, he will use the Bible many times to help us understand how far we had gone from the Word of God and His plan of eternal love for us. Also the children will express their hurt and sufferings due to the poor communication skill we'd show them and also how difficult it was for all of us to talk about our feelings and sensations. Anyhow, the sessions lasted almost a year and I think that it helped us very much. My husband was impressed with the Word of God and the results of listening to it as a family which later on helped him to join the Church and decided to walk with us. The fights became less and less frequent and we would all enjoy the few moments of peace and quiet. My sons were very involved in the music program at School and thank God they were always busy and practicing their instruments and getting ready for the next concert would take most of their time. The few free hours that they have, they will play ball in the backyard or see their friends.

For the first time in my married life, I had a few years of bliss and happiness beyond what I have ever had with my husband and sons, well perhaps when Ray and I started going out and falling in love. I didn't know then that alcohol will destroy our relationship in such a way and only after we joined the Church and began to be guided by the Holy Spirit, I learnt of my traumas and my incapacity to love the "other" or what the church identifies as the enemy. Jesus died for us so that we could love the other as he/she is, without judging or trying to be right all the time. St. Paul says that to be a Christian is to be another Christ "Christ leaves in me and I in Him" "it is Him who acts not I". This principle is also used by all the 12 steps programs and it is called "detachment". In the christian life you do not detach yourself from the problem but you take upon yourself the sins of the other, you let go and let God fix the wrong which we had made and not trying to get justice but to let your opponent be.

I am a "woman of little faith" if any, but I must admit and declare that my life has been changed completely upside-down, if God didn't do it then I don't know who. I can tell about the changes in my life, I can be a witness of His actions and interventions, because I have been there and experienced it. Things which were impossible for me to do least to conceive, had happened. I am certain that God exists and that He changed my history, the direction of my future. I remember then, after we reconciled, we went to see the movie 'Back to the Future", and I could understand the story very well because I have had something very similar done to me and my sons. We have come back and a new future was opened for us. We have experienced a "bad" past but given the chance to start anew, start again, live a new life. How many families will have that experience… to come back from the negative to the positive, from "slavery to freedom" says The Word regarding the reason for having the Eucharist in the Catholic Church. Eucharist means Celebration, extreme and fantastic Feast were everybody present (if they agreed) may be changed, renewed, taking by the strong Arm of The Lord from slavery to freedom, from death to Live, in a moment, any moment during the celebration your life may changed for the better, and receive the strength to become a Christian, a child of God. To be touched by the Holy Spirit can be turned into a new creature, born again as some of the protestants say when they have been transformed when accepting our Lord Jesus Christ as their Saviour and giving themselves to Him. I have received such a gift. The resurrection. To be passed from being dead to becoming alive again, to be given a second chance!. I cannot express myself any clearer and louder than this. I was watching a TV program this morning were a family had recently had a loss, a brother has passed away because of cancer, and the sister wanted to celebrate with a party the first anniversary of his death while the mother of the young man, wanted to celebrate an anniversary Mass for the repose of his soul according to her catholic beliefs. The conductor of the Program agreed with the sister of the dead man and told her not to worry about the religious ceremony because it wasn't that important. My point here is that that mentality is growing at all levels in this society and it is first, lack of knowledge of our roots and a total rejection of our traditions some religious and some not. We spent millions of dollars seeking customs and religious ceremonies of diverse tribes and native nations. It is very popular to see the Media, particularly TV, visiting ancient places and explaining to the viewers intricate rituals and precise details while our catholic traditions passed to us by the apostles, ancient prophets and many faithful writers are being ignored and mercilessly criticized while we are not teaching our children their roots and the faith which is vital and a priority to find happiness and the wellbeing we are all entitled to.

I happened to read a biography of this wonderful Pope and believe in his integrity and the love he felt for The Lord, made him a friend of "the People of God" and unable to cause any damage to them. I'm glad that I am finding information on his defense and I am also happy to be able to add this piece to My Life. This is some of God's plan of Salvation from the constitution on the Sacred Liturgy of the Second Vatican Council ('1964): "As Christ was sent by the Father, so in his turn he sent the apostles, filled with the Holy Spirit. They were sent to preach the Gospel (Good News) to every creature, proclaiming that we had been set free from the power of Satan and from death by the death and resurrection of God's Son, and brought into the kingdom of the Father. They were sent also to bring into effect this saving work that they proclaim, by means of the sacrifice and sacraments that are the pivot of the whole life of the Liturgy. So, by baptism men are brought within the paschal mystery (which comes from the Jew's history) Dead with Christ, buried with Christ, risen with Christ, they receive the Spirit that makes them God's adopted children, crying out: Abba, Father; and so they become the true adorers that the Father seeks." Volume II Liturgy of the Hours, Second Week of Easter (second reading) Saturday, Office of Readings. This is what gave the Pope Pius XII the power and the will to save this Jews putting his life in danger for them and it the same Spirit who gave me the power the will and the intention to forgive my alcoholic and abusive husband, to forgive him and reconcile with him through the distance of our two countries and four years of separation and the divorce papers being issued and the case closed. The Spirit that is in His Church and that it is given to us through the Sacraments as needed. I am a witness to that and a member of the Church, the Body of Christ.

Pope Leo the Great, now a saint (Epist. 28 ad Flavianum, 3-4: PL 54, 763-767) says: "Lowliness is assured by majesty, weakness by power, mortality by eternity. "Wise words which we can say that are true and they are because we understand and know lowliness, weakness and mortality. These words are used in our Language, exposed in our Dictionary (ies) and touch in our Universities, Schools and Colleges and off course we also use and understand and accept majesty, power and eternity but I am not sure of the last one...do we really understand "Eternity" or use it at all or know it well enough to apply it in our daily life and affairs but I don't think that we use it in that familiar way as perhaps we should because Eternity exists and even science cannot deny its existence. The point is not the words or its meaning but the comparison that Pope Leo the Great has exposed in this particular document. In the United States of America the word "majesty" is not well appreciated or understood for obvious reasons which we are not going to discuss now, while power is much used and understood in our democratic system and way of life but do we get the meaning "weakness is assured by power"? I am not sure we do but is Pope Leo the Great aware of his statement? I believe so but I wanted to write about an article which appeared in the AARP Magazine of Spring 2012 and here are the parts of it that I think has to do with the Pope's statement in the past centuries:" Whatever happened to civility? Is an often heard lament, particularly among those of us over 50 who recognize civility's increasing absence in a world changing at warp speed. Technology has forever altered the style, speed and reach of our decidedly less personal communication. Escalating vulgarity, lax standards, sensational media and polarized politics reign. Society today is far different than it was when we were young. While rudeness is pervasive and rising (one recent report concluded that bad behavior may be the "new normal"), the societal and financial costs of incivility are astronomical-impacting our homes and relationships, schools, economy, health care and government. Civility is more than polite courtesies. Derived from the Old French and Latin term for "good citizen," civility enables us to live respectfully in communities; it is the glue that binds our society. It can be the difference between life and death- as, for example, when health care professionals bully subordinates, cover mistakes and create mistrust." Good for Pope Leo the Great! He was talking about how to act civilly, which is "practicing kindness, generosity and gratitude. Substantial research shows" continues the AARP article "that people who regularly engage in these acts live longer, healthier and happier lives." Well now we know the basic steps to live better and happier lives and it all starts with "Lowliness" which means Humility a word that comes, as I wrote before in this book, from the Latin word

"Hummus" (earth, soil, dust, ground) so let's have our feet firmly on the ground and act civilize and things could change. The problem is that kindness comes from love, gratitude is a virtue as it is generosity and virtues come from a higher source as the Church teaches, so we are back where we started....Love is God and God is Love and we cannot have one without the other. If we don't accept God or don't know God we won't know or accept Love. The Church is there for us to receive this love which is Jesus's own Spirit. This is the "technique" of the process if you want to call it that: Jesus (the Word) is preached to us, if we accept Him we will receive the Spirit which will make us Christians (like Christ) and, as Christians, we could love and be kind and practice generosity and feel gratitude and so on....Civility without Jesus Christ who is the builder, the instrument used by the Creator, His Father, to create the world and all that it contains. The document from Pope Leo the Great continues: "He (Jesus) who is true God was therefore born in the complete and perfect nature of a true man, whole in his own nature, whole in ours. By our nature we mean what the Creator had fashioned in us from the beginning, and took to himself in order to restore it. He took the nature of a servant without the stain of sin, enlarging our humanity without diminishing his divinity. He emptied himself, though invisible he made himself visible, though Creator and Lord of all things he chose to be one of us mortal men. Yet this was the condescension of compassion, not the loss of omnipotence. So he who in the nature of God had created man, became in the nature of a servant, man himself" This great pope explains it beautifully and in a very convincing fashion. It convinced

me and many more before me and it would continue on changing the face of humanity because that is what the son of God does.

Philly, PA 08/18/2015 We have to start over...Convert-turn back to the Lord and believe in the Gospel! I believe therefore I spoke" This is real, we need must announced that The Kingdom of God is near (is coming to us) The disciples always said "The Kingdom of God is coming with us" like the famous country song "Go tell it to the mountains" Tell everyone, go anywhere repeats pope Francis constantly that Jesus Christ is true! He is here as Head of the Church, The Messiah, the Son of God, King of the Universe, the one we have been waiting for, the Savior Emmanuel, the only one with joy says one of the psalms from the Bible, Life eternal if we listen to Him, accept Him as our Lord and Savior and follow. With this faith, the faith of his followers, the Church, we must begin to evangelize or re-evangelize as the people whom Jesus is calling to do so. After I heard in a catechesis (the teaching of the Church-The Kerygma) The Gospel showing those who are called to form part of the Church, the facts of the risen son of God by the power of the Holy Spirit, my life and the life of my sons changed completely and we went to another direction, came back to California and to the Church, part the family started to look for changes in their lives and some found the door to a good life. A life of service and care for the other through the Church. Our older son Christopher married in the Catholic Church and he and his wife both open to life are parents of ten (10) children and are grandparents now, the younger son became a priest and is attending a Parish and a Seminary in the east of the USA. Some more members of the family came back to the Mother Church and are serving in Missions around the country and also in Spain. Four of our grandchildren go to Church every week and some of them sing during the Service. The last popes called it "Missio ad gentes" and this humble service done as a response to God's action/intervention on our lives, has helped many persons who have been far from the Church and from God, some for many years, as I was.

My Life 1-29-2012 (Baby boomers II)

I wanted to say more about the "baby boom" generation and its great influence on my life because the world was very much involved with them (us) in more than one way. Our presence in all areas of society meant a great deal about decision making, marketing choices, financial enterprises and more...In my experience I must say that I was very much directed by their presence and the powerful impact that their particular way of thinking made on everything that they will get involved with. Most of the choices they made during those years, have been the basic style of thought for the present generation and even our actual financial situation might has its roots in their way of thinking, and I think this because we don't get ideas from cero (0) but from waves which circulate from mind to mind, from one individual to many and once they (ideas) are created, they do not stop but continue in an innuendo of force which penetrates in all the areas of our inner being and if not rejected or sorted out, they would begin impregnating the complexity of our psychic, until we finally accept them without question. So that is how I was also involved in some of the ideas of my generation and, as part of the baby boomers, I became a self-made projection which would stay with me during the most important years of my life. I realize now, after being awaken from my sleep, that all those high ideas made a big different in my thinking and my decision of leaving my husband and take his children from him in secret, was a part of that egoistic thinking were our "freedom" was more important than our values and our choice had to be honor and, as I heard from areas which were important to me, do anything that would make you happy not matter what! There, that was the motto, the center of the philosophy which has been created by the selfish baby boomers, to do whatever you wish to please yourself and with that many husbands were cheated, many homes were abandoned and many children separated from one or another parent. I know that many people suffered terrible because of my choice (the movie "Sophie's Choice" comes to my mind) because it was a terrible choice with terrible consequences which some members of my family are still suffering from. God made the family, He created the bond of marriage and made it sacred because it is and only He can separate it as many formulas used to perform marriage ceremonies say, and if we break these vows, these promises said at the altar, we are making a mistake which would go into the future and destroy it. I've seen it happening to me and many more people and as the statistics confirm every day, one of every 10 marriages, ends in divorce. Why? because marriage comes from Heaven as the perfect institution for a family to form and to grow to become a Christian family and beget Christian children who would grow up to be Christian adults who would beget more Christian children. To act against this secret union means to fight God's creation and the future of many families and many children would be uncertain without these facts being taken seriously and to the letter as it was intended. I speak from my own life and my experience, and because I've been there done that, I have the authority to write about it and express it as I've seen in my life through my wrong choices brought upon myself by my generation who acted and decided without God because they would not have the vision or the knowledge of Him in their lives at all. I had some knowledge of God because when as a young girl my mother would take my brothers and sisters to Mass and even though she would not stay (she said she was always busy) we would go in the church and attend Mass and see the priest and everybody doing some kind of worship to some kind of divine presence and it made a difference in me. That experience I had in Spain the country were I was born, but here in the USA and other countries, the secularization had already started, so the rejection of God was already very strong during the baby boom generation and that made the type of society which was the base for the next one which is the 80's and the 90's generation which was if I can remember properly, when the drugs started to be heavily used by almost every body and in every area in the structure of the so called "the world that we live on" and I don't write this in judgment because it is a new way to survive to become numb or changed by all kinds of chemical altered products which also alter our natural beings and made them into something we are not. The good The news is that there is a new way to live and that is the Christian way, taking upon ourselves the new nature of the "new man" who has received a new Spirit who happens to be the third person of the Trinity who is the one God. The new creature (born again) who is capable of performing the actions that humanity needs to survive in the new life and it is to love the other as they are, and just by performing that impossible act, we can change situations and live the happy life which we need to live, and that was created for us. I was fortunate to find the Church or better yet, to be found by God and brought to Church because my life was turned around and I was given a second chance and I know that not everybody gets it, and because of that, I am now writing this pages hoping that I can finish my book and published and God willing, somebody else may receive the chance of a lifetime.

This is something which I read during morning prayer and the Seventh Week of Easter, it goes like this: "After Christ had completed his mission on earth, it still remained necessary for us to become sharers in the divine nature of the Word. We had to give up our own life and be so transformed that we would begin to live an entirely new kind of life that would be pleasing to God. This was something we could do only by sharing in the Holy Spirit". This is what I've experienced and the "sharing" it is done in reference to The Church, The Assembly because Church means Assembly, since Church in Spanish means Ecclesia which comes from Latin for Reunion or Assembly. When we gather to worship, pray and share the body and blood of Christ we form an assembly and we might receive the Holy Spirit if we believe that It is with us. The Spirit which He (Jesus) left with The Church so that It could be guided and instructed by Him (the third person of the Holy Trinity) One God, Three persons. The information that I'm giving above is from a commentary on the gospel of John by Saint Cyril of Alexandria, bishop and it can be found on page 990 volume II The Liturgy of the Hours. That is one of the prayer books which we use in The Neo- Catechumenate or The Way as it is called. In page 982-983 of the same volume, second reading which is taken from the dogmatic constitution on the Church of the Second Vatican Council and this is what it says: "The Spirit dwells in The Church and in the hearts of the faithful as in a temple. He leads the Church into all truth and gives it unity in communion and in service. In this way the Church reveals itself as a people whose unity has its source in the unity of Father, Son and Holy Spirit". Well it can not be put clearer than that! And I'm so glad that I've found these readings during morning prayer. This is what

I've been writing about but I think that I needed some support and I thank God that I've found it. One of the many experiences that I have had since I've entered the Church is the action of the Holy Spirit which I could receive in the Sacraments if I want to receive it. It's all about God respecting our freedom so much that He always waits for us to want Him to accept His Spirit in our lives and be changed or transformed by Him and this incredible question is asked to us along our Itinerary of faith and we respond what we are willing and ready to receive or to give up for our new lives to become a reality and The Second Vatican Council brings forward into the renewal of the Church" He leads the Church into all truth and gives it unity in communion and in service". This truth is one of the many which were accepted by me during my indoctrination and now I'm living a life of communion in the Church Community and service as I'm serving the Church wherever I might be sent to do whatever needs to be done during this particular time of my life. So because of my present condition and situation which I've accepted as the History that God is making for me, I am able to understand this truths as something that it can be done as God takes it into effect and makes it possible for me to live a life of service and sharing for the good of The Church and for the Glory of God.

Eternal Father, I don't understand Eternity but I know it's there waiting for me, for all of us since you love all Humanity and because it's there I need to go reunite with you and the rest of the saints who are already with you. My life needs to be directed towards Heaven and towards You, My Father, my Creator and my God and I also need to tell others the Good News, that Eternity exists, that You are real and that everything that the Church has been teaching us since Christ funded it it's the truth and nothing but. The world needs to be funded on these facts and Faith has always been the beginning of all wisdom and the meaning of Life itself. When the world believes, everything makes sense and Life would give us the answers which we need to survive but there was a gap in history and revolutions and the first thing that the rebels did was to attack the church and kill Christians because behind every rebel there is the number one rebel, the Devil himself. Does this make sense? because it does to me and to other members of the Church who also believe in him. Now, after I've come back to the bosom of the Church, my life needs to be oriented towards Heaven, towards Eternal Life and that is what the Church teaches us and what Jesus Christ told us. He came to earth to tell us precisely that we have a Father who loves us and that we have been created by Him and for Him and that He gave us a soul and will give us His Spirit if we want it and if we choose to be on His side. Some members of my family think that I might be losing my mind even when I've told them that I was coming back home and to my husband, they did not understand and did not agree. I think that I've already talked about it and let me tell you that coming back wasn't easy and I still remember that we were stopped at the Barajas Airport because my sons were illegal as I'd never registered them at the US Embassy. My mother cried and begged like never before. I begged and I might also have cried, the boys just waited scared and all the time all these people followed us and begged the Barajas's police officer to let us go. The brother of one of the members from my first Church community who was employed by TWA at that time, accompanied us to the ticket counter and intercede for us to the Captain of the airport police, also begged for him to let us go. All of us prayed very hard while he reminded me of the crossing of the red sea by the Israelites and I started to think of it. Somehow I thought that God would open the sea for us and suddenly it happened and the Captain of the police all of a sudden told one of the officers to take us to the plane…to the plane!!!!! I just couldn't believe it and being a "woman of little faith" continued with my children towards the plane gate and the beginning of our new life. There had been many miracles in my life but I think that this has been one of the greatest and it will always be in my memory and in my heart and I've told many people this event and I would continue to share it because it is the truth and because God wants the Glory and the credit for His Mercy.

Today Memorial Day and maybe because of that, maybe for some other reasons, I've been remembering my husband all day (long) and it's been good to remember…I remember because, not only he was a person worthy of being remembered but because he was a soldier, a very good and obedient soldier and he deserves to be remembered in such a Day as this. I remembered his smile, his sweet and gentle eyes, his voice and all the things which a husband is remember (ed) for. I particularly thought about the time when he was chosen to be the responsible of our Church Community. There was a group of 62 people of all ages and we had a wonderful retreat for a weekend and everybody was very happy and full of joy. I know now that it was the Joy of the Holy Spirit whom very few people acknowledge nowadays, even Church goers. Two of our young members have had their First Communion during the retreat and we had a great celebration being witnesses to these two people receiving communion for the first time and because of it, adult members for ever unless they reject the faith later on. I haven't seen those two people for a long time but I know that, whenever they might be, they would always remember that moment. After the retreat was almost over and a "Christian" community was formed, came the time to vote for a responsible and some brothers and sisters who would be chosen to help him, anyhow these people who are chosen (by secret vote) to serve and help the Community is called the Responsible Team and we chose one after some of the candidates were substituted by those who had the most votes. I remembered that when my husband was asked by the catequists if he was willing to accept, he turned his head towards me and told me: why do you get me involved in this? And what am I going to do as a responsible member of a Community? My answer was: "it not the people who had elect you but God Himself and you can't you shouldn't say no to God, don't you think?" After this, he turned back to the catequists and said: "yes I accept" just like any great political or religious figure would say "I accept"; then the catequists asked me if I accept to support the responsible everyway I could, and I said: "yes". That is the part that I remember more clearly and today remembering I smile. I wanted to go to a local cemetery and pray in memory of my husband together with all the American soldiers that died serving the country but I didn't and went shopping for summer clothes instead. The bus that I was riding passed by a small cemetery where someone had taken some flowers and as the bus was passing, I said a prayer for him. Al together a memorable and patriotic Memorial Day. I thank God for the fact that even though many countries are battling against famine, inside and outside wars, hatred and racism, here in the U.S.A. we enjoyed a peaceful and quiet day.

Approximately during Fall of 1983 and after my reconciliation with my husband, I started to prepare our trip back to USA (my two sons and

I remember our excitement and joy; both my sons were eager to see their father and to come back to their country even though I knew that they'd worry about the future and being back with their father caused them some amount of stress and living Spain and the protection of the family would not be easy for them. I've told them to trust in The Lord and that The Church was also in California and that it will help. That put them at ease and the thought of having our own community in the States and being able to listen to The Word helped them immensely. Christopher, then 11, is the oldest and he could take more responsibility for his actions and I also noticed that he'd remembered his father better than his brother Michael who was more uneasy than him. Anyhow, I know now that God made time go faster than usual and soon we were ready to go back putting our future in His Hands. The company where I worked for almost a year decided (in a providential way) to provide me with a "vacation check" to compensate me for the time that I did not use for seeking leave and with that generous amount I used to purchase our plane tickets. On the day of the trip we said our goodbyes to the family and took a taxi to the Barajas airport which was then half the size of the modernized actual one, but on the other hand and because it was smaller there was also more security and there was even a police station situated near the entrance to the exit gates, where one of the biggest miracles of my life took place. I've talked about this many times as a testimony of how God intervenes when necessary. This is what happened: The Chief of police had been notified by one of the agents who checked our passport that there had been an error in our traveling papers. My son's had been added to my passport in the Spanish consulate in the US but because of the time spent there was more than the allowed for foreigners, they should've been registered at the American Embassy at Madrid which I didn't do. I was shocked by this news and told him that I wasn't aware of this legality and that I was sorry. While I was explaining myself, tears started rolling down my cheeks as I started to plead and beg to let us go and at the same time one of the agents of the TWA airlines situated at the airport who was a relative of one of the sisters of our Spanish community, started also to beg to the chief of police calling him by his first name, also to "let us go" while telling him and all the people who has gathered near the station's glass door, about our divorce four (4) years ago and our reconciliation happening during the past months. The chief of police was moving his head and giving us all kinds of reasons why he would not let us go, lifted up his head, called one of the police agents waiting around and told him to take us to the nearest American Embassy. The children and my mother started crying and sobbing while begging him to please be gentle and to let us get together with my husband. Suddenly the chief of police called the agent back, a perplexed look on his face, and pointing to the gate and in a soft voice, told him to take us to the plane which was waiting just for us. Later on somebody told us that the pilot had waited for almost 8 minutes, something unusual for Spanish punctuality. I took my sons by their hands, kissed my mother goodbye and run to the exit blessing and thanking The Lord for such a wonderful deed

My Life 02-09-2012 (life after surgery)

God gave us a present, based on our past to take us into a new future and I don't know exactly how it works but I know that's what He did to gives a second chance, and it doesn't have to be a "near death experience" to make it happened just to be in the right place at the right time which means, to be a seeker of the truth, be truthful yourself and it would happened and I'm not saying that you are to live a life of fantasy and total joy but you are going to find the LIFE capital letters. My husband forgave me and took me back and a few months later, he fell ill. When he suffered the first heart attack, it was a hot summer day, he was mowing the lawn of what was still our house, in the suburbs of Fresno, a nice country town in the central valley in the state of California. He was sweating, drinking a beer and smoking a cigarette (he used to smoke a packet of Wiston everyday) . I was sitting by the back porch watching him and I saw him bend over while his face showed an excruciating pain in process. I stood up immediately and ran towards him helping him to sit on the steps of the back door and I remembered asking him if he wanted me to call an ambulance and when he said yes, I hurried to the phone. Five minutes later, the team who came took him to the hospital after they checked his vital signs and realized that he was having a heart attack. I jumped on the front with the driver trying to keep calm and prayed hard for his life. God heard my prayers because he was able to have surgery a few days later, receive a multiple bypass and the surgery was a success even though the doctors said that his heart had suffered irreversible damaged and that he should be put on the list of heart recipients and wait for a new heart but my husband, my beautiful husband had some reservations on the subject and refused to even be put on the list. He survived the complicated surgery for 11 years, went back to college and received his Bachelor's degree just because he didn't want to be in the house doing nothing. I supported his decision, accompanied him as much as I could and assisted to daily Mass and also became a member of the AA (Al Anon) meeting which helped me to cope with his alcohol withdrawal syndrome which made him go crazy sometimes because he had to stop drinking on the advice of his doctors. Going to this international support group helped me in all areas of my life and made possible my relationship with my husband and my somehow confused teenage sons. Even their acceptance of their father's illness and difficult situation was much better than I expected. I suffered very much during my husband's illness and the time that he spent in the hospital was not easy for my sons and I. The fact that my mother had come to visit during that time made it possible for me to visit Carl and I would spend as much time with him as I could. I took care of the bills, took the family to the park, shopped for groceries and kept going the best that I knew how. Two of my brothers-in-law are nurses and also my husband's only sister, so I would get a lot of professional advice and support from them. Carl was back home after a few weeks and I expected a lot of changes for us, not only at the table but in every area of our lives but thank God, was able to accommodate my time to his and very slowly his recovery started and as we all got involved in the process, our lives became more and more real, communication was better and the house was like a small clinic were care and attention was given 24 hours a day. When my husband became stronger, he became a coach for our sons and enjoyed his time with their activities while my sons also received the attention that they needed in their lives, when we were not in the right mind to give them to them. May God be praised forever for His tender mercy's to us.

LESSONS FROM CHURCH WHY?

The Church, as our Mother, imparting to us a new identity in the love and holiness in which she herself was formed, also has the responsibility of teaching us, of forming us ever more perfectly in the new identity we have received (through baptism) not from the world but "from above" I should explain: "the duty of the pastoral teaching of the Church is aimed at seeing to it that the People of God abides in the truth that liberates "and the truth will set you free. After I left my husband, (I have been planning to run away for a year, I went to my family in Spain to seek for shelter and support and stayed with them. My mother was angry at me because she was very fond of him and was convinced that I was at fault. I thought that I was right before I encounter the Church, later the announcement "Kerygma" changed my thinking inviting me to convert (believe in the Gospel) This is what the the Catechesis for the world meeting of families says: "Christian spouses are not naïve; know life's problems and temptations. But they are not afraid to be responsible before God and before society. They do not run away, do not hide, do not shirk the mission of forming a family, and bringing children into the world… Of course it is difficult! That is why we need the grace that comes from the sacrament. Grace is giving to marriage strong, giving the spouses courage to go forward, and without isolating oneself but always staying together. Christians celebrate the Sacrament of Marriage because they know they need it. This new identity in this chapter is the new creature that is given to all the baptized. It was given to me but it was not revealed and nurtured because I've left the church in my youth. I have begun to receive the instruction, the teachings and the bread that comes from Heaven. My husband and I married in the Catholic Church, yes but it was convenient at the time. Carl Martin, my husband, a sergeant stationed at the Air-Force base of Torrejon de Ardoz near Madrid, the capital of my country, Spain, and I met there. I was working at the base Library and I always had the idea that it was love at first sight as it is said, and maybe it was. After the birth of our two sons, Carl was giving orders to be stationed in a small town in Germany and we lived there for a year or more. It was there in Germany that I decided to leave him for the first time. The reasons for my decisions are not important now. I would only say that I thought I had had enough.

 I would try to explain why we need to remain and belong to the church as a baby attached to his/her mother. Close to her receiving the nourishment that it needs. This love in which we're born in

Christ is a love we cannot give ourselves. One received, some little by little (the way of conversion) some all at once. (St. Paul in his way to Damascus) it is purifying, so that the church, in the person of each of her sons and daughters, is constantly being transformed in Christ's love until Christ is fully formed in all of us (the baptized/members of the "mother Church" (church meaning assembly) gathered by God Himself the body of Christ (His bride) with Christ Himself as head (the) this is the meaning of the image of the pilgrim church, a church "on pilgrimage" towards her final perfection, perfection in and by the very love that defines her in the first place. ???

Phila....08/09/2015

My visits to St. Teresa of Jesus or Teresa of Avila as we called her in some regions of Spain, have produced an extraordinary change in my soul. After the last visit I purchased the TV series and enjoyed washing it very much. I learned so much of her personal relationship with the Lord, that invited me to begin a relationship with him too. I understood somehow that Teresa saw Jesus not only as the Lord but as a man, and as a man she treated him. Sometimes she would get angry at him and scold him almost as a wife does to a husband. Theresa is one of several Doctors of the Church and very much respected not only in Avila and Spain, but in many parts of the world. This is one of her deep thoughts: O Lord, take into account the many things we suffer on this path for lack of knowledge! The trouble is that since we do not think there is anything to know other than that we must think of You, we do not even think of You, we do not even know how to ask those who know nor do we understand what there is to ask. Terrible trials are suffered because we do not understand ourselves, and that which isn't bad at all but good we think is a serious fault.

Just as cannot stop the movement of the heavens, but they proceed in rapid motion. So neither can we stop our mind. "(from the collected works of St. Teresa of Avila – volume 2 The interior Castle IV:1)

Fresno, 12/01/2015- ASH WEDNESDAY…a Mystery.

Religious celebrations are strange and exotic, others so familiar that they must as well be made at home. Which are which depends on your experience and practice. Contrary to social events, Christians celebrations are all performed as part of a common ritual which is chosen as a Liturgy. Ash Wednesday, the beginning of the Lenten season, is a day of fasting and rejoicing celebrated as part of the great Easter cycle in the Catholic tradition. First we must remember the original meaning of Lent, the church's holy spring in which catechumens were prepared for baptism and because of it, penitents were made ready by penance. The ashes traced on the form of a cross upon their foreheads is not only a sign of repentance for sins but a reminder of the death and resurrection of our Lord Jesus Christ.

The ashes on the forehead of a Christian also shows the turning of minds and hearts to God in preparation for the celebration of the Paschal Mystery in during which some will be baptized while others will be restored to the communion of the faithful, everyone renewing willingly the consecration of their lives to Jesus Christ.

The cross traced with the blessed ashes on the penitent forehead during the celebration of Ash Wednesday, is the sign of Christ's victory over death. The words said by the minister while marking the penitent's forehead 'Remember that thou are dust and to dust thou shall return" are a perfect reminder of the challenge to spiritual combat at baptism: dying with Christ, Christians may also rise with Him.

Ash Wednesday is a day in which joy and grief go together hand in hand. The penitent receives a smear of ashes but also the promise of purification, preparing him for the cleansing waters of Baptism or the sacrament of penance. Having been freed from sin allows the clear air of God's spring, the sunlight of Easter Sunday (The day of the sun) shines upon us and purifies us.

In some monastic communities, monks go up to receive ashes barefooted for, feeling the floor or the ground under your feet is a also a reminder of the simplicity of life.

The Liturgy of Ash Wednesday is, for people who know what it means for their souls to be absolved freed from guilt. A joyful event to celebrate, is like a calm sea of Mercy, as in Him (Jesus) there is no anger while the ashes being blessed and sanctified by the sign of the cross, become a health giving grace bringing cleanness to the body as well as protection to the soul, availing for the remission of sins. They also bring the pardon which the penitents are seeking, receiving the ashes.

Agnes Martin

G. Edwards English A

9 August 1990

John XXIII A Pope for All

I have chosen to present a research paper about Pope John XXIII because I admire humbleness in a person with power, and I recognize it as a sign from God.

Pope John XXIII successor of Pius XII (John 1419) was a spiritual father to millions of people. I used to think that being holy or saint was the same as being good but, I was wrong. You can be a good saint or a bad saint, a good priest or a bad one, and the same process applies to any person. John XXIII was a good person and therefore he was a good Pope "he remained meek and humble of heart, no matter what the personal sacrifice" (Capovilla 130).

Pope John was a saintly priest recognized as such by all who knew him for his gaiety, piety and love of mankind:

This book reveals the intimate feelings and true character of a man and priest whose transparent goodness enabled us to catch a glimpse of an inner life rich in the beauty of holiness (Journal xv) "the whole life of a priest who became Pope, and reveals what he kept a jealously guarded secret behind his smiling and innocent gaiety" (Capovilla xvi).

His piety made him accessible to other men. People called him the good Pope, everyone's Pope, the Parish priest of the world. He persuaded men to pray, to ponder the Gospels, to reform the morals of the world by reforming themselves (Journal xviii) "I wanted to love God at all costs and my one idea was to become a priest, in the service of simple souls who needed patient and attentive care (Journal xvii).

Born on the 25 of November, 1881, Angelo Giuseppe at Sotto il Monte, Bergamo (Italy), he was of peasant stock (Journal 227). He was elected Pope October 28, 1958 and 90 days after, he put reforms into practice (Catholics 502). He was acting in promoting social reforms for workers, the poor, the orphans, and the outcast (John 419). His poverty impressed public opinion, was a consolation to the poor (Journal xix) "I am poor, thank God, and I mean to die poor" (Elliot 200), and also "Who will ever forget his kindly glance, his marvelous smile, his warm voice, which was so quick to extend a welcome?" (Capovilla 5).

In 1959 Pope John announced plans for an ecumenical council. This was being done so that the church could walk towards new ways of feeling, wishing and behaving" words spoken by Pope Paul VI while inaugurating the 2nd session of the Ecumenical Council (L'Osservatore Romano 30 Sept 1963). Vatican II opened in October 1962, ended in Dec 1965 and has been influencing the lives of catholics ever since "the whole world anxiously longs for this liberating spirit of agreement which will prepare the triumph of justice in the life of the nations' ' (Roncalli 65). "So Vatican II came…it began by boldly opening the church to new currents in the world." These words were spoken by E.G. Brown, former Governor of California about the results of the council (Catholics 505), and "but, as Pope John XXIII hoped when he convened Vatican II, there has been a great rebirth" (Catholics 514), comments made by Charles W. Whalen Jr., former Republican member of Congress representing the third district of Ohio, and currently president of New Directions, Washington, D.C.

Pope John XXIII a man for the church but also a man for the world, became Time's 'Man of the Year' and the fulsome article proclaimed: 'To the entire world Pope John has given what neither diplomacy nor science could give, a sense of the unity of the human family' (Hebblethwaite 468).

And of course the beautiful words of his successor and admirer Pope Paul VI "This was John XXIII: Blessed be this Pope who has made us enjoy the world. Every one of us has felt the charm of this man and has understood that the affection which surrounded him was sincere; it was no fashionable enthusiasm nor was it inspired by superficial motives. It was a secret which revealed itself to us, a mystery which absorbed us; it was perhaps a perfectly simple combination of two qualities, truth and charity, which shone with its magic power before our amazed and delighted eyes" (Sullivan 99).

What else could I add to this sincere recollection of facts? This was indeed John XXIII, a Pope for all. He also died a saintly death (Hebblethwaite 417) or, "You are dying like a wise man, a sincere christian…(Capovilla 137).

'True love permit us to serve the other not out of necessity nor vanity but rather because he or she is beautiful above and beyond mere appearances …"The poor person when loved is esteemed as of great value and this is what makes the authentic option for the poor differ from any other ideology from any attempt to exploit them for one's own personal or political interest." Citing St. John Paul II, Pope Francis added: "Only this ensure that" "in every Christian community the poor feel at home." "Today, radical feminism and a secularized culture make the concept of humble service (free) somewhat incomprehensible, as taking the last place willingly, as it is letting others have the credit for a job well done- such acts are seen as servile, demeaning, even unhealthy. On the contrary, when we accept the yoke of service "in imitation of Christ ", who was gentle and humble of heart, we cannot lose but gain "gratis" the Kingdom of Heaven. (8-11-2015 Feast of St. Clare sister of the poor.)

chapter about Love and Christians. Cited from an article by sister Constance Veit Director of communications for the Little Sisters of the Poor (. Magazine Columbia) Notes about Blessed Junipero Serra: It is important to know where he was born (in the village of Petra Mallorca, Spain) from a family of farmers in 1713, he attended the Franciscan school. At age 18, he joined the Franciscan Order and took the name Junipero after one of the first companions of St. Francis of Assisi. Ordained at 25 he became a theology professor five years later. When he heard about the need for missionaries in the New World, Fray Junipero asked permission for this service. Disembarking in the city of Veracruz, he chose to make the 250ml. trek to Mexico City by foot firmly confronting the dangers of such a difficult and unknown journey, during which one of his legs became swollen due to an insect bite, a wound that would plague him for the rest of his life. Having learned the native language, he translated prayers and catechisms and taught the faith and celebrated rich Liturgies. (Sacraments) Also during this time he worked hard to improve the living conditions of the natives introducing farming, crafts and trades, ways to bring fresh drinking water to the Mission, etc. By the time he was recalled to Mexico City eight years later, most of the natives had become practicing Catholics and their way of life improved in every way.

In 1767, when King Charles III abruptly expelled the Society of Jesus from Spain and its colonies, Serra was named president (administer) of the Jesuit Missions in Baja California. Soon after arriving, he was informed of Spain's plans to safeguard the Alta California coast by establishing missions from St. Diego to Monterey. It was an opportunity he had longed and prayed for –to plant the faith on untilled soil (farmers expression) – he immediately volunteered to "erect the holy standard of the cross in Monterey."

Archbishop Gomez (Archdiocese of Los Angeles, California) says: "I think Blessed Junipero Serra is a great example for Catholics everywhere. He dedicated his life to the mission of evangelization, to bringing the "Good News" –to the poor- especially to the people of California and the rest of America by his example and works of faith. He understood that the mission of the Church is to bring others to the love of God. As to know God is to love Him and to love the other as yourself. The other is Christ…

Fray Junipero was a very smart person, well prepared and well educated, still he decided to leave everything behind and come to an unknown place with the idea in his heart to save alms. This decision to leave everything was just an incredible leap of faith. During St. John Paul II visit to Mission St. Michael, he recalled the "heroic deeds of Fray Junipero Serra…the Apostle of California."

About Purgatory and what it means for us after our passing: 08/12/2015 - Father Nieremberg, of the Company of Jesus (Jesuits) who died in the odor of sanctity at Madrid –Spain- in 1658, relates a fact that occurred at Treves, and which was recognized, says Father Rossignoli (Merveilles, 69), by the Vicar General of the diocese as possessing all the characteristics of truth. On the Feast of All Saints, a young girl of rare piety saw appear before her acquaintance who had died some time previous. The apparition was clad in white, with a veil of the same color on her head, and holding in her hand a long rosary, a token of her devotion towards the Queen of Heaven. She implored the charity of her pious friend, saying that she hah made a vow to have three Masses celebrated at the altar of the Blessed Virgin Mary, and that, not having been able to accomplish her vow, this debt added to her sufferings. She then begged her to pay it in her place. The young person willingly granted the alms asked of her, and when the tree Masses had been celebrated, the deceased again appeared expressing the joy and gratitude

Meanwhile time passed, and, notwithstanding the Masses and prayers offered for her, that holy soul remained in her exile, far from the eternal Tabernacles. On December 3td, feast of St. Francis Xavier, her protectress going to receive Communion at the Church of the Jesuits, the apparition accompanied her to the Holy Table, and then remained at her side 'during the whole time of thanksgiving, as though to participate in the happiness of Holy Communion and enjoy the presence of Jesus Christ. On December 8th, feast of the Immaculate Conception, she again returned, but so brilliant that her friend could not look at her. She visibly approached the term of her expiation. Finally, on December 10, during Holy Mass, she appeared in a still more wonderful state..After making a profound genuflection before the altar, she thanked the pious girl for her prayers, and rose to Heaven in company of her guardian angel.

Some time previous, this holy soul had made known that she suffered nothing more than the pain of loss, or the privation of God; but she added that "that privation caused her intolerable torture. This revelation justifies the words of Saint Chrysostom in his 47th Homily:" Imagine, he says, all the torments of the world, you will not find or equal to the privation of the beatific vision of God."

The pain of loss, in which we now treat is, according to all the saints and all the doctors, much more acute than the pain of sense. It is true that, in the present life, we cannot understand this, because we have too little knowledge of the Sovereign Good for which we are created; but, in the other life, that ineffable Good seems to souls what bread is to a man famished with hunger, or fresh water to one dying with thirst, like health to a sick person tortured by long suffering;

it excites the most ardent desires, which torment without being able to satisfy them.

The church gives the name "Purgatory" to this the final purification for the elect, which is entirely different from the punishment of the damned. The Church formulated her doctrine of faith on the Purgatory especially at the Councils of Florence and Trent. The tradition of the Church, by reference to certain texts of Scripture, speaks of a cleansing fire.

"As for lesser faults, we must believe that, before the final judgment, there is a purifying fire. He who is truth says that whoever utters blasphemy against the Holy Spirit will be pardoned neither in this age nor in the age to come. From this sentence we understand that certain offenses can be forgiven in this age, but certain others in the age to come."

"Here, I would say, stands the controversial point and the difficulties posed by the method of the members of the Neocatechumenal Way. From what one sees, they come and apply, to the letter, a method born and prepared in Europe, without caring about adapting to the local world. I've found among them here in Japan the same style that I saw in Cameroon, where I was a missionary twenty years ago; the same songs (with the guitar), the same expressions, the same catechesis, all transmitted with a style based more on imposition than proposition. One can thus understand the tensions, disagreements and reactions they generate, which sometimes find them little disposed to dialogue. Their intentions are certainly admirable, their good will, but insertion in the local culture is missing. This, in my modest opinion, is what the local Japanese bishops are asking of them - to take off the European dress in order to present the heart of the message in a purified way close to the people."

Bottari, 69, is today the pope's ambassador in Hungary.

Along with the new documents, *La Repubblica* also published a note, allegedly written on a computer by one of the Vatican insiders leaking the texts, which insists that the papal butler arrested in late May is merely a "scapegoat" and that the real authors of the affair are to be found within the "central power" of the Vatican.

The note appeared to suggest the leaks would continue, insisting the leakers have "hundreds" of documents in their possession.

The Vatican spokesperson, Jesuit Fr. Federico Lombardi, appeared resigned to seeing the revelations continue, in remarks to reporters during the pope's weekend visit to Milan for a World Meeting of Families.

"We do not expect that the documents published so far will be the last," Lombardi said. "It's clear that those who have accepted this quantity of documents will use them with their own strategies and for their own purpose, certainly not with the intention of doing everything at once and then leaving us alone."

We see in the Revelations of the saints that on Saturday, the day specially consecrated to the Blessed Virgin, the mother of God, she descends into the dungeons of Purgatory to visit and console her devoted servants. Then, according to the pious belief of the faithful, she gives relief and consolation to those souls who have been particularly devout to her. If such takes place on an ordinary Saturday we can scarcely doubt that the same occurs on feast days consecrated to her. Among all her festivals, that of the glorious Assumption, the Blessed Mary delivers several thousands of souls. Needless to say that to believe in the Mother of God is a must as it is believing in Purgatory as a place where all who pass away without being purified first, will go to "purge" a number of years or perhaps days according to the extreme and seriousness of their sins. The Catholic (Universal) church teaches this as a place to wait until the souls are ready /pure enough for Heaven. (Purgatory explained by the lives and legends of the saints by Fr. F.X. Schouppe, Editorial TAN Books Charlotte, N. Carolina)

Why Are We Baptized? If we believe that Christ has died for all, meaning in the name of all representing the head of Humanity, we need to know that what it's of great value before God is the obedience for love signifying the sacrifice of a life totally donated. The faithful, made willingly participating in death by baptism (submerging in the Baptismal font means for the Christians dying to original sin as the beginning of a new life in Christ) accept/ratified the oblation of Christ and his offering as a victim in the cross. St Paul writes in his letter to the Romans:" Are you failing ignorance? Don't you know that all who have been baptized have been baptized in his death? We had been buried through our baptism in his death so that as he resurrected from among the dead for the glory of God his father, so also we will live a new life. Paul continues in Romans 6,4 "Baptism does not oppose to faith, on the contrary it accompanies and expresses We know that our old self was crucified with him, so that our sinful body might be done away with, that we might no longer be in slavery to sin. We know that Christ, raised from the dead, dies no more. Death no longer has power over him. He is alive and lives for God Consequently you too must think (by faith) as being dead to sin (by baptism) and living for God in Christ Jesus. Baptism has destroyed sin in men, but while our bodies have not been dressed in immortality, sin could still be living in the "mortal" body and the spirit of Jesus (the immortal life) would not. Therefore Baptism berries the body of sin which comes up as a new man member of the body of Christ and the One Spirit. This resurrection would not be total and definite until the end of times. This rite which is one of the (seven) sacraments in the church, is presented in the NT as a bath that purifies and gives life as a new birth with the possibility to start anew (Noe's ark was a type of baptism) (1@Peter 3,21)

but he is not totally sure about the jet. He explained himself in a very child like way:" children go near their sport favorite hero and want to be near him or her, surrounding them with their affection and attention. Just like Jesus want us to love Him, to wish to be with Him, put Him first in our lives, come to Him when He is near and enjoy His words, his company.

Speaking of Heaven, the retribution of God from Heaven is being revealed against the ungodliness and injustice of human beings who in their injustice hold back the truth. For what can be known about God is perfectly plain to them, since God made it plain to them Rm 2:4 or are you not disregarding his abundant goodness, tolerance and patience, failing to realize that this generosity of God is meant to bring you to repentance? Your stubborn refusal to repent is only storing up retribution for yourself on that Day of "retribution" when God's just verdicts will be well known. "He will repay everyone as their deeds deserve."

Philly 09/01/2015 About being Christian.

A Christian is someone else, St. Symeon the New Theologian (+ 1022) once wrote, "When a man walks in the fear of God he knows no fear, even if he were to be surrounded by wicked men. He has the fear of God within him and wears the invincible armor of faith. This makes him strong and able to take on anything, even things which seem difficult or impossible to most people. Such a man is like a "Giant surrounded by monkeys" (book by Fr. Pious E. Sammut OCD

Discalced Carmelite first edition) By the way, that book's intention is to show us the way to be "like giants" in and through Jesus Christ.

To me Jesus Christ is like a giant, He can do anything. That is what the team of catechists in Madrid told me when I asked them the same question as the disciples of John the Baptist came to ask him after the encounter with Jesus: "What do I do now? Shall we follow Him or stay with you? John said "Follow Him". My catechists told me "Ask your husband for forgiveness" And so I did and he forgave me, no conditions, no fear whatsoever, it was for me a fantastic experience, a real Miracle! God has been preparing my husband for my letter letting him know that I was sorry, that I had been wrong and caused him much pain and suffering. I was honest and he believed my words in the letter. He called me and I told him that if he forgave me I would go back home. He was moved and he forgave me by phone. A picture could be made from this event and it is a real story, a true story. My life, the family life started anew. God gave us all a new life, an opportunity of reconciliation between all of us and all the members of the family benefited by this Yes! The Church once more has mediated and, through the Sacrament of Penance/Reconciliation, saved my family and my immediate family from disaster. Jesus, the Giant, the Kyrios, the King of the Universe, the son of God, has had mercy on us or our situation. The Church asked me if I was disposed to let Him act in my life, to save my marriage and He did.

We need to put just a little bit of God into our life, even a tiny speck, (the parable of the woman and the yeast) and God's life will open your existence up wide and you will become more and more the person God intends you to be.

Philly - 08/28/2015

In the Way we say that, the presence of Jesus Christ is to be found in the Gospel (Good News) Christ says: "Love one another as I have loved you. In this, they (those outside of the Church) will know that you are my disciples" (Jn 13:13: 34-35) Attention to "as I have loved you" because it is the foundation: the stone the builders rejected has become the corner stone" A special love is needed. I do not, Joseph continues in his book "The Kerygma ", if you ever seen this kind of love made present, made flesh, made a sacrament, a sign. "Love as I have loved you!." How has Christ loved us? Christ loved us when we were his enemies, when we were sinners, evil. It is love for the enemy. Have you ever seen a Christian that loves his enemy? Where is that kind of love? Where can this love be seen? Because Christ says: "Love as I have loved you. In this way they will know that you're my disciples". In this dimension of love to the enemy.

So that in a community (the Church -the Assembly gathered by Christ himself) this kind of love could be seen, it is absolutely necessary the Christian Community instructed and initiated in an itinerary of Faith and by the grace of the Holy Spirit. Also to be able to pass the faith to our children it is essential to receive it first and give the signs of love and unity required in the Gospel.

Philly 09/02/2015.- The Christian is someone else. That statement implies the definition many are unaware of. A Christian is not just someone who follows Christ or becomes another Christ or Christ like, even a baptized person; no. It defines very well what it is :Someone else, someone that looks like us, eats, sleeps, walks, marries, loves, dies, etc. but it does not think like us nor reacts like us. "And I do tell you, at least you become like these children, you will not enter into the Kingdom of Heaven." Do we really understand this advice, this warning… Do we know what the Kingdom of Heaven is, how is it formed, created, who is the king of such a kingdom, who are its subjects? I asked a young man that I know, he is studying to become a seminarian (someone who is being prepared, educated to be a priest, even though the Church gives these seminarians the freedom to leave the seminary any time. The Church in its wisdom and the authority given by God, has the role to be a loving mother who admonishes and also choose those who have received the vocation to the priesthood before being ordained and, even after being ordained, these men still might change their minds and choose marriage or single lives. This person, this candidate, explained the Kingdom of Heaven compared to a place; a high and special place where there is a king and subjects of course. It may even be Heaven but he is not totally sure about the jet. He explained himself in a very childlike way:" children go near their favorite hero and want to be near him or her, surrounding them with their affection and attention. Just like Jesus wants us to love Him, to wish to be with Him, put Him first in our lives, come to Him when He is near and enjoy His words, his company.

Speaking of Heaven, the retribution of God from Heaven is being revealed against the ungodliness and injustice of human beings who in their injustice hold back the truth. For what can be known about God is perfectly plain to them, since God made it plain to them Rm 2:4 or are you not disregarding his abundant goodness, tolerance and patience, failing to realize that this generosity of God is meant to bring you to repentance? Your stubborn refusal to repent is only storing up retribution for yourself on that Day of "retribution" when God's just verdicts will be well known. "He will repay everyone as their deeds deserve."

8/27/2015

Philly - why believe? -About Faith and Baptism-

"In a moment, in the twinkling of an eye, as the final trumpet sounds, for the trumpet shall indeed sound, the dead shall rise incorruptible and we shall be changed." Paul's letter to the Corinthians is indicating here that the gift of that future change will be given to those who, during their time on earth are united to Him (Jesus Christ) and his companions by upright lives within the communion of the Church. In order then, that men may obtain the transformation which is the reward of the just, (they) must first undergo here on earth a change which is God's gift. Those who in this life have been changed from evil to good are promised that future change (conversion) as a reward.

This is the secret of your formula (referring to the Neo-catechumenate) which provides religious assistance, a practical training in Christian faithfulness, and effectively integrates the baptized into the community of believers which is the Church. The person who has been baptized needs to understand, to think over, to appreciate, to give assent to the inestimable treasure of the Sacrament he has received like a seed that has not yet developed.

The name Catechumenate and it,s intention does not invalidate or diminish the baptism currently received but its intention is to renew and practice with time the intensive method of the treasure of the sacrament he has received as a child.

We are happy to see that this itinerary of Faith is being received in parishes all over the world, saving separated families, baptized people far away from the mother Church, funding new seminaries where many young men are being educated and formed to become priests for the near future Church.

Pope Paul VI says: "To live and foster this re-awakening is what you call a kind of "post baptism", which can renew in our contemporary Christian communities the effects of maturity and depth which were achieved in the early church during the period of preparation before baptism. You do this afterwards. Whether before or after is secondary, I would say. The fact is that you aim at the authenticity, fullness, coherence and sincerity of Christian life."

Pope St. John Paul II says: "We (the Church) have a need of faith, of great obedience to the Church. This radicalization of faith is needed, yes, but it must always be situated within the life of the Church, and with her guidance, because the Church in her entirety has received the Holy Spirit from Christ in the persons of the apostles after His resurrection…This joy that surrounds you, that is in your songs, in your behavior, may very well be a sign of your southern temperament, but I hope it is a fruit of the Spirit. I believe that is the Spirit who initiates this way."

From 1 Corinthians 15:29-31

Otherwise, what are people up to who have themselves baptized on behalf of the dead? And what about us? Why should we endanger ourselves every hour of our lives?

Rm 3:27-31

Rm 6:1-11 "Baptism"

Philly 09/08/2015 Related to the existence of God: If God does not exists who has created us?, the World, complete with oceans, seas, lakes, rivers, mountains, all its reaches, etc. Then animals, all species, kinds and rituals. After all these were created (from nothing) comes men. This incredible perfect machine with the intelligence to investigate, think, discover fantastic, the gift to reason, decide freely, etc. Yes the theory of the famous "Big-Bang" is accepted by many professors and scientists but this is not invalid according to God's creation. The Vatican is accepting this manner of the world being created and even maybe the animal evolution is possible to a reasonable point of a higher power involved in this way of creation. The Bible does not specify the "modus Operandi" of such a great endeavor, on the contrary it supports it.

Philly/16/2015

For the Church, the true one the church that welcomes the unwanted, the lonely, the rejected, the sick, the dying, the needed, the widows, the homeless and better yet, the murderers and the unloved, all are welcome! in the present world and the other, as long as we repent and accept the Lord to be gestated in us. When 'the church's prophets sent by her through the inspiration of the Holy Spirit, announced the Good News "The Kerygma" to me, I said yes like his Mother the Blessed Virgin Mary, and through faith I believed that what these angels (messengers) were saying in the name of the Church and immediately I started to think different, something in me changed (I believed so I spoke) as the scripture teaches. By the Sacrament of Penance -Reconciliation, my sins were forgiven and the process of conversion started like an embryo in the womb of the Church, the first thing I did was to go to the catechists who had given the announce of Jesus Christ forgiven all my sins and loving me as I am. I asked them what I was to do next and they told me that If I trust God to get my family together. I told them "Can God do that? My husband is in California and I'm in Spain. Their answer entered into my heart like an arrow straight ahead: "Is there anything impossible for God? By going back into Church and believing in the Gospel, my life turned in another direction and towards the plan that God had already prepared for me and the family. So I did what they told me and prepared to come back together with my sons. In a letter I asked my husband for forgiveness and to my surprise, he did, by phone! Victory for Jesus. I has been freed from slavery to freedom and a heavy weight has been taken off my shoulder. My sons were happy to come back and accepted without asking any questions except if they were to recognize Dad right away. I reassured them that they will. The three of us have been liberated from the grip of the evil one whose influence has made us get away from the right path. I was hoping that The Lord would keep helping us along the way. The catequistas told me that Carl would accept me and I knew that he loved his sons, that was good enough for now.

This is my personal experience. A unique encounter with God in the person of His son Jesus Christ whose presence (substance) as Joseph says in his book "Kerygma" I recognized while listening to the catechesis given to me and a group of people in the 80's in a Parish in Madrid. I had been separated from Carl for 3 years when he sent me divorce papers through legal procedure. I happily sent the papers back and considered myself free from bondage, but God had other ideas and when the catechists (A team of several members of the Way who've been walking enough to be able to give these catechesis-announcement to other people that need it or are in a situation where there looking for answers. When I understood what god wanted from me I read to listen to them. when I asked them what to do there answer was to ask my husband for forgiveness and my question was how am I going to do this since he is in California and I am here in Madrid, there response was is there anything impossible for the lord that would entire into my heart and I responded immediately and wrote a letter to my husband asking him to forgive me and that I have found an answer for us, the answer was forgiveness. Would he be able to forgive me? And I left it up to him to make the next step. I wrote a letter in obedience to the church and to the group of catechists, but I wasn't sure he would forgive me after what I have done to him. To my surprise he responded by phone two weeks later and I told him if you forgive me I will come back. He responded yes I forgive you, bring me my sons whom you took away from me. I went back to the catechesis and told them, he just told me he wants his sons, he doesn't want me. My catechesis said to take your sons to him and he would want you too. And it happened. After our phone conversation, I talked to the children and told them what had happened and that we were going back home to California. My sons would have followed me anywhere at that time since they trust me not to fail them though I've left a couple of times already but always come back for them. I began to prepare for the trip and it took me 4 to 6 mo. to get ready. When this happened I was working as a secretary - adm. in a very important company and was making good money.

Philly 09/14/2015

Still in the famous city of Philadelphia in the old state of Pennsylvania, trying to cope with the day as it comes. In this month of September, people from everywhere are being called to meet the Pope during his visit to the city of "brotherly love".

Philly PA 09/11/2015: The Eucharistic Sacrifice.- We have seen the High Priest coming to us; we have seen and heard him offering his blood for us. We priests follow, as well as we can, so that we may offer sacrifice for the people. Though we can claim no merit, we are to be honored in the sacrifice; for although Christ is not now visible offered, yet he is himself offered on earth when the body of Christ is offered. Moreover, it is made clear that he himself offers in us, since it is his words which sanctify the sacrifice which is offered.

Explaining Sacrifice: The American Heritage Dictionary (Based on the new Second College Edition) says: The offering of something to a deity,. The forfeiture of something highly valued for the sake of someone or something considered to have a greater value or claim.

The Perfect and Acceptable sacrifice.- We are the true high-priest family of God. God himself bears witness to this, when he says that, everywhere among the Gentiles, sacrifices are offered to him well-pleasing and pure. Now God receives sacrifices from no one except through priests. Anticipating all the sacrifices we offer through his name –the sacrifices Jesus Christ enjoined us to offer in the Eucharist of the bread and cup- the sacrifices now offered by Christians everywhere throughout the world -God bears witness that they are well pleasing to him.

Persons can be in a truly interpersonal relation to one another only by sharing something in common. Without communion, there can be no friendship and communion in the Greek culture is based on the term "Koinonia" and if the "koinonia" is one of common values and shared convictions, this can be the basis of a friendship in the most genuine sense of the term.

Philly 09/03/2015 Purgatory explained:

The Dogma of Purgatory is too much forgotten by the majority of the faithful; the Church suffering, where they have so many brethren to succor, whether they foresee that they themselves must one day go, seems a strange land to them. This truly deplorable forgetfulness was a great sorrow to St. Francis de Sales. "Alas!" said this pious doctor of the Church, "we do not sufficiently remember our dear departed; their memory seems to perish with the sound of the funeral bells."

The principal causes of this are ignorance and lack of faith; our notions on the subject of Purgatory are too vague, our faith is too feeble.

Giuseppe Moscati (Doctor Italiano (Santo ?)

A veces subestimamos el poder de recuperación del cuerpo humano hecho a imagen y semejanza de Dios. Y olvidamos sobre todo el poder sobrenatural de la oración hecha con fé.

Fresno 11/17/2015 - Christians who wish to escape the rigor of Purgatory must love the mortification of their Divine Master, and beware of being delicate members under a head crowned with thorns. On February 10, 1656 in the province of Lyons, father Francis of Aix, of the Society of Jesus, passed away to a better life. He carried all virtues of a Religious to a high degree of perfection. Penetrated with a profound veneration towards the Most Blessed Trinity, he had for particular intention in all his prayers and mortifications, to honor this August Mystery; to embrace by preference those works for which others showed less inclination, had a particular charm for him. He often visited the Blessed Sacrament, even during the night, and never left the door of his room without going to say a prayer at the foot of the altar. His penances, which were in a manner excessive, gave him the name of "The man of suffering". Another fault against which we must guard, because we so easily fall into it, is the notification of the tongue, Oh! How easy it is to err in words! How rare a thing it is to speak for any length of time without offending meekness, humility, sincerity or Christian Charity! Even pious persons are often subject to this defect; when they have escaped all the other snares of the demon, they allow themselves to be taken, says St. Jerome, in this last trap-slander-. Everything we do, how we act and/or respond, has its consequences which may lead us to make more serious mistakes, errors and even grave sins. The Church, our Mother (The Mother of Jesus) teaches what to do to choose Heaven, but first we must be directed towards It as we are passing through enemy territory and taking the wrong route can be dangerous and fatal. Christians who are convinced of such Mystery being true, will be attacked with more fury than they expect and would need to take refuge under the protection of our Savior who is always waiting for us to ask. "Ask and shall be given to you" pure and simple put into words by the Master Himself. Just ask, He is telling us even to the point of making this advice easier for anyone, He says: "when two or more are reunited in my name, ask and everything will be given to you". Marxism had the illusion that social justice and the globalization of the economy would solve the problems that were encountered in those times. That illusion has vanished. 'The poor needs justice not Charity!" Marx exclaimed in this new doctrine. The Church social justice, as the perfect expression of Christian Faith, "Give to Caesar what is Caesar and to God what is God's" has revolutionized the world and the forgives of sins had liberated man from slavery, not just by not having a master but by being given the possibility of becoming a child of God, another Christ.

Philly 08/30/2015

About my life as a sinner and how I changed gradually through the action of The Word (proclaimed in the Liturgy of The Word) every week. About the gifts of the Spirit I want to let you know that, when I was a pagan I was irresistibly drawn to inarticulate heathen gods. Because of that, it's quite clear that no one who says a curse on Jesus can be speaking in the spirit of God, and nobody is able to say "Jesus is Lord" except in the Holy Spirit. (1 Co 12:1-4)

Hardships develops perseverance, and perseverance develops a tested character, something that gives us (the Christians) hope, and a hope that which will not let us down, because the love of God has been poured down into our hearts by the same Spirit (the third person of the Holy Trinity which has been given to the Christians (adults with faith).

Philly 09/03/2015: This year Pope Francis has asked consecrated persons to "wake up the world" with their "prophetic and countercultural witness." This might sound like a tall order- but religious life is, by its very nature, countercultural. For us Little

Sisters of the Poor, giving the kind of witness our Holy Father is calling for means being faith to the spirit of our foundress. (written by Sister Constance Veit L.S.P. in a column published in Columbia Magazine April 2015)

We need to understand that "Consecrated" means dedicated to God. Since St. Pope Paul John II wrote to the whole Church in Evangelii Gaudium (The Joy of the Gospel) "True love is always contemplative, and permits us to serve the other with that love seeing in the need the face of Jesus Christ. We receive this unconditional love from God through His son, and share it with the other, "our neighbor" here it comes the commandment "Love thy neighbor as yourself" which is, in Jesus's own words, the fullness of the Law. Pope Francis has called this year "The Year of Consecrated Life " and because of it has asked already consecrated Christians and those who are to be consecrated to "wake up the world" as his motto. By doing acts of Mercy and Charity in silence, taking the last place, serving the poor, mostly the needy. Mother Theresa of Calcuta (already beatified) said to a reporter who asked her the reason for the sisters of charity wanting to fund a convent of her order in the city of San Francisco, and her response was: The poor are not only those who lack food, or those in the streets, but also the lonely and this country is full of them. We came to help all the poor and to see Jesus in them. What we do to them we do for Jesus. (look for the reading in the Scriptures…..)

I've already written why the Church? Why is it here among us? Now I'm asking What is the Church? " I'd tell what I know: "Church –the word church in latin – Spanish means Ecclesia –Iglesia – Asamblea The first asambla –Assembly was gathered in Jerusalem, called for by the first leader perhaps the Apostle James (Santiago) a cousin of our Lord. Or maybe the first pope Peter- Simon whose name was changed by Jesus to Peter – piedra in spanish rock in the English language.

In this first Assembly, the organizing of the sending of the disciples to accomplish our Lord's command: "Go and announce to my brothers, to the lost sheep of the house of Israel, that the Kingdom of God, the Kingdom of Heaven is near." That is what Probably happened according to the writings of the fathers of the Church.

Philly 09/24/2015

About Christ, sin, the origins of the world and Paradise.

Christ reconciled the world with God with His own blood (do we understand, really why the sacrifice?) Jesus Christ belongs to the Hebrew race (?) same ethnicity as well as a member of the Jew nation/people. We must remember what performing sacrifices meant to them, what the building of altars were to place the victim on, kill it, therefore take his life, offer it to a god, such victims were sometimes burned (therefore the term "burned offerings". This was done not only by the Hebrew nation but also by many peoples from other cultures and nations would share the same or similar rituals to offer to their gods/idols even to the point to of forcing the natural law, with the intention to placate them or please them for their own protection or to have a plentiful harvest.

We have heard of the origins of creation until we know the known world. Christians believe that God (Yahweh) the creator, separating the then unruly waters from land, made the light, ordered darkness to remain in a selected place away from the light, at the same time providing clean and proper air for our survival, beasts and animals of all kinds, greenery and trees, jungles, prairies, deserts, mountains and everything needed for a world in perfect order and harmony according to its needs and to God's will and pleasure.

09/19/2015

Philly - why believe? -About and Baptism-

"In an instant, in the twinkling of an eye, as the final trumpet sounds, for the trumpet shall indeed sound, the dead shall rise incorruptible and we shall be changed." Paul's letter to the............ is indicating here that the gift of that future change will be given to those who, during their time on earth are united to Him (Jesus Christ) and his companions by upright lives within the communion of the Church. In order then, that men may obtain the transformation which is the reward of the just, (they) must first undergo here on earth a change which is God's gift. Those who in this life have been changed from evil to good are promised that future change (conversion) as a reward.

This is the secret of your formula (referring to the Neo-catechumenate) which provides religious assistance, a practical training in Christian faithfulness, and effectively integrates the baptized into the community of believers which is the Church. The person who has been baptized needs to understand, to think over, to appreciate, to give assent to the inestimable treasure of the Sacrament he has received like a seed that has not yet developed.

The name Catechumenate and its intention does not invalidate or diminish the baptism currently received but its intention is to renew and practice with time the intensive method of the treasure of the sacrament he has received as a child.

We are happy to see that this itinerary of Faith is being received in parishes all over the world, saving separated families, baptized people far away from the mother Church, funding new seminaries where many young men are being educated and formed to become priests for the near future Church.

Pope Paul VI says: "To live and foster this re-awakening is what you call a kind of "post baptism", which can renew in our contemporary Christian communities the effects of maturity and depth which were achieved in the early church during the period of preparation before baptism. You do this afterwards. Whether before or after is secondary, I would say. The fact is that you aim at the authenticity, fullness, coherence and sincerity of Christian life."

Pope St. John Paul II says: "We (the Church) have need of faithers, of great obedience to the Church. This radicalization of faith is needed, yes, but it must always be situated within the life of the Church, and with her guidance, because the Church in her entirety has received the Holy Spirit from Christ in the persons of the apostles after His resurrection…This joy that surrounds you, that is in your songs, in your behavior, may very well be a sign of your southern temperament, but I hope it is a fruit of the Spirit. I believe that is the Spirit who initiates this way."

Phila….08/09/2015 Regarding Faith

My visits to St. Teresa of Jesus or Teresa of Avila as we called her in some regions of Spain, have produced an extraordinary change in my soul. After the last visit I purchased the TV series and enjoyed it very much. I learnt so much of her personal relationship with the Lord, that invited me to begin a relationship with Him too. I understood somehow that Teresa saw Jesus not only as the Lord but as a man, and as a man she treated him. Sometimes she would get angry at him and scold him almost as a wife does to a husband. Theresa is one of several Doctors of the Church and very much respected not only in Avila the rest of Spain, but in many parts of the world. This is one of her deep thoughts: "O Lord, take into account the many things we suffer on this path for lack of knowledge! The trouble is that since we do not think there is anything to know other than that we must think of You, we do not even think of You, we do not even know how to ask those who know nor do we understand what there is to ask. Terrible trials are suffered because we do not understand ourselves, and that which isn't bad at all but good we think is a serious fault. Just as cannot stop the movement of the heavens, but they proceed in rapid motion. So neither can we stop our mind." (from the collected works of St. Teresa of Avila – volume 2 The interior Castle IV:1)

Philly 09/12/2015 About Baptism (cont.)

The church, as our Mother, imparting to us a new identity in the love and holiness in which she herself was formed, also has the responsibility of teaching us, of forming us ever more perfectly in the new identity we have received (through baptism) not from the world but "from above" I should explain: "the duty of the pastoral teaching of the Church is aimed at seeing to it that the People of God abides in the truth that liberates-"and the truth will set you free.-After I left my husband, (I have been planning to run away for a year, I went to my family in Spain to seek shelter and support and stayed with them. My mother was angry at me because she was very fond of him and was convinced that I was at fault. I thought that I was right before I encounter the Church, later the announcement "Kerygma" changed my thinking inviting me to convert (believe in the Gospel) This is what the Catechesis for the World Meeting Of Families says: "Christian spouses are not naïve; know life's problems and temptations. But they are not afraid to be responsible before God and before society. They do not run away, do not hide, do not shirk the mission of forming a family, and bringing children into the world... Of course it is difficult! That is why we need the grace that comes from the sacrament. Grace is to make marriage a strong fortaleza, giving the spouses courage to go forward, without isolating oneself but always staying together. Christians celebrate the Sacrament of Marriage because they know they need it. This new identity in this chapter is the new creature that is given to all the baptized. It was given to me but it was not revealed and nurtured because I've left the church in my youth. I have begun to receive the instruction, the teachings and the bread that comes from Heaven. My husband and I married in the Catholic Church, yes but it was convenient at the time. Carl Martin, my husband, a sergeant stationed at the Air-Force base of Torrejon de Ardoz near Madrid, the capital of my country, Spain, and I met there. I was working at the base Library and I always had the idea that it was love at first sight as it is said, and maybe it was. After the birth of our two sons, Carl was giving orders to be stationed in a small town in Germany and we lived there for a year or more. It was there in Germany that I decided to leave him for the first time. The reasons for my decisions are not important now. I would only say that I thought I had had enough.

I would try to explain why we need to belong to the Church and remain in her as a baby attached to his/her mother, being close to her receiving the nourishment that babies need. This love was given to us when we were born in Christ and it's a love we cannot give ourselves. Once received, some little by little The Way of conversion-catechumenate, some all at once (St. Paul in his way to Damascus) it's purifying so that the Church, in the person of each of her sons and daughters, is constantly being transformed members of the "mother Church" (church meaning Assembly) gather by God Himself and the body of Christ/His Bride with Christ himself as it's head. This is the meaning of the image of the pilgrim church, a church on "pilgrimage" towards her final perfection, perfection in and by the very love that defines her in the first place. My visits to the convents renewed by St. Teresa of Avila as she is known in some regions of Spain, have produced an extraordinary change in my soul. After the last visit, I purchased the famous TV series on her life and enjoyed very much to know more about such a great saint. I learned so much of her personal relationship with the Lord that invited me to begin a relationship with Him also. Somehow I understood that Teresa saw Jesus not only as the Lord but as man, and as a man she treated Him. Sometimes she would get angry and scold Him like a wife does to a husband. Teresa is one of the several Doctors of the Church known until now and very much respected, not only in Avila and Spain but in many parts of the world. This is one of her many deep thoughts: O Lord take into account the many things we suffer on this path for lack of knowledge! The trouble is then, since we do not think there is anything to know other than we must think of You, we do not think of You, we do not even know how to ask those who know nor do we understand what there is to ask. Terrible trials are suffered because we do not understand ourselves, and that which isn't bad at all but good, we think is a serious fault. Just as we cannot stop the movement of the heavens, but they proceed in rapid motion, so neither can we stop our mind". (from the collected works of St. Teresa of Avila-Volume 2 "The interior Castle IV: 1

09/23/2015: About the Canonization of Fray Junipero Serra Today. (by Pope Francisco)

'True love permit us to serve the other not out of necessity nor vanity but rather because he or she is beautiful above and beyond mere appearances ..."The poor person when loved is esteemed as of great value and this is what makes the authentic option for the poor differ from any other ideology from any attempt to exploit them for one's own personal or political interest." Citing St. John Paul II, Pope Francis added: "Only this ensure that" "in every Christian community the poor feel at home." "Today, radical feminism and a secularized culture makes the concept of humble service (free) somewhat incomprehensible, as taking the last place willingly, as it is letting others have the credit for a job well done- such acts are seen as servile, demeaning, even unhealthy. On the contrary, when we accept the yoke of service "in imitation of Christ ", who was gentle and humble of heart, we cannot lose but gain "gratis" the Kingdom of Heaven. (8-11-2015 Feast of St. Clare sister of the poor.) chapter about Love and Christians. Cited from an article by sister Constance Veit Director of communications for the Little Sisters of the Poor(. Magazine Columbia)

Notes about Blessed Junipero Serra: It is important to know where he was born (in the village of Petra Mallorca, Spain) from a family of farmers in 1713, he attended the Franciscan school. At age 18, he joined the Franciscan Order and took the name Junipero after one of the first companions of St. Francis of Assisi. Ordained at 25 he became a theology professor five years later. When he heard about the need for missionaries in the New World, Fray Junipero asked permission for this service. Disembarking in the city of Veracruz, he chose to make the 250ml. trek to Mexico City by foot firmly confronting the dangers of such a difficult and unknown journey, during which one of his legs became swollen due to an insect bite, a wound that would plague him for the rest of his life. Having learned the native language, he translated prayers and catechisms and taught the faith and celebrated rich Liturgies. (Sacraments) Also during this He worked hard to improve the living conditions of the natives by introducing farming, crafts and trades, ways to bring fresh drinking water to the Mission, etc. By the time he was recalled to Mexico City eight years later, most of the natives had become practicing Catholics and their way of life improved in every way.

In 1767, when King Charles III abruptly expelled the Society of Jesus from Spain and its colonies, Serra was named president (administer) of the Jesuit Missions in Baja California. Soon after arriving, he was informed of Spain's plans to safeguard the Alta California coast by establishing missions from St. Diego to Monterey. It was an opportunity he had longed and prayed for –to plant the faith on untilled soil (farmers expression) – he immediately volunteered to "erect the holy standard of the cross in Monterey."

Archbishop Gomez (Archdiocese of Los Angeles, California) says: "I think Blessed Junipero Serra is a great example for Catholics everywhere. He dedicated his life to the mission of evangelization, to bringing the "Good News" –to the poor- especially to the people of California and the rest of America by his example and works of faith. He understood that the mission of the Church is to bring others to the love of God. As to know God is to love Him and to lead the other as yourself. The other is Christ…

Fray Junipero was a very smart person, well prepared and well educated, still he decided to leave everything behind and come to an unknown place with the idea in his heart to save souls. This decision to leave everything was just an incredible leap of faith. During St.

John Paul II's visit to Mission St. Michael, he recalled the "heroic deeds of Fray Junipero Serra...the Apostle of California."

Philly 09/17/2015

About sacrifice: Every work that affects our union with God in a holy fellowship is a true sacrifice; every work, that is which is referred to that final end, that ultimate good, by which we are able to be in the true sense happy. As a consequence even that mercy by which aid is given to man is not a sacrifice unless it is done for the sake of God. Sacrifice, though performed or offered by man, is something divine; that is why the ancient Latins gave this name of "sacrifice", of something sacred. Man himself, consecrated in the name of God and vowed to God, is therefore a sacrifice insofar as he dies to the world in order to live for God. Works of mercy, then, done either to ourselves or to our neighbor and referred to God. This too is part of mercy, the mercy that each one has for himself. Scripture tells us: Have mercy of your soul by pleasing God.

My book is almost finished and I am glad because writing it was difficult and heavy sometimes but, please don't get me wrong! Because I had a great time writing it and putting it together even though I know that I'm going to need help to complete it and of course to edit it and publish it. God would be praised by my life experience being exposed and explained here and I really hope to have it published and for many people to read it and to benefit from my decision to write it. Three priests suggested for me to write about my life and another one supported these priests' suggestion. One of them is my son who is a very good Priest according to what a person (very well known in the neocatechumenal way) said about him and I agree, not just because I am his mother and love him but because it is true. He is a very good priest and loves the

Lord with all his heart and that makes him a special person to be able to dedicate himself to the service of people of all kinds. My sons are both nice and good and I thank God for giving them to me, allowing me to be their mother and having them for all these years. Today I wanted to talk about people who give their life for the church and are witnesses of the Love of God and His presence among us. I wanted to write about an article which I came across during this Easter time. The article exposes some of the help that Pope Pius XII gave to the Jews when they were being persecuted and hunted down from the Nazis. I owe my life to the Pope ``is the title of this interesting article by Herman Herskovic and the part that I would like to expose says this: "They were terrifying days. The old boat was like a box of matches. Everyone had to remain quietly in his or her place. If ten people got up to move around at the same time, the boat would have capsized. In Istanbul, a police craft prevented us from entering the port to replenish our food and water supplies. After having traversed the Bosphorus and the Dardanelles, we reached the Aegean Sea. The misadventures were not over. The boiler did not stand up to the strain and cracked. The ship wandered for hours before striking against the rocks of an island and sinking. By swimming we reached the shore. For eleven days, our only food was raw fish. We were then collected by an Italian ship and transferred to a prison camp on the island of Rhodes. From there, some of my companions were able to contact family members at home. The father of one of my comrades obtained the freedom of his son, with permission to travel to Switzerland. During his journey to the north, the young man stopped in Rome and was received in the audience by Pius XII. To the Pope he recounted all of our story and he also told him also of our fears due to the presence of German troops on the island of Rhodes. Pius XII listened attentively to him and promised his intervention with the Italian government. Two weeks later, we were transferred to a safer concentration camp in Calabria. When the allies *landed in Sicily, the Church intervened to help us. Toward the Germans, despite everything, I do not feel any excessive anger, because I think that the majority of the population was misled. I know however for certain that the many people, in many places, did not help the Jews. It is not just to accuse Pius XII for something that was not under his control. Personally I owe him a great deal and I thought it was right to tell." This story defending the person of Pope Pius XII and his help and concern for the Jewish people during the Nazi reign of terror appears as part of a Documentary title Pope Pius XII: Friend and Rescuer of Jews and tells the story of hundreds of Jewish refugees shipwrecked in the Aegean Sea, who turned to Pope Pius XII for help and got it. The story is written by William Doino Jr. and it appears in the January 2012 number of The Inside the Vatican magazine and I has been looking for testimonials on the matter since I.*

AND THOUGHTS

Last night enjoying the beautiful fireworks and celebrating the 4th of July surrendered by all those cheerful people, I remember my husband, my sons when they were boys looking up at the serene sky of Fresno and I smiled while watching the splendid lights which crisscrossed the firmament while the suave water of the Hudson river was made to shine and pastel colors kept flashing in front of our eyes. I've also remembered all those soldiers young and not so young who had missed this celebration all those years spent away from home doing their duty defending this country so attacked and criticized by people and countries which do not understand the USA. Now I understand better about feeling patriotic, loving the American spirit and giving your life to defend all those values which had made this country great. But there is a danger of taking the wrong turn towards selfishness and indifference and that could be fatal and wrong because this country still needs values the same values that made us what we are, and those are the Judean-Christian values and teachings which had drawn the maps of time and had designed our pass and our future, our destiny as a people; our duties as a Nation. All that I was thinking last night while looking up and admiring the colors of our flag being transformed into fireworks sending a strong message to everyone who was standing there waiting and showing with their presence that they were proud Americans too and that they loved this country. What an ending for that special day! Yes, we need to bring back respect for our elders, love of life from the moment of conception (no exceptions) , the sacred love shared and created between a man and a woman (no exceptions) , leadership for our youth and a clear picture of our role in the world. Somebody has to stop this madness and put some moral order to work and it's not going to be China so I am hoping and praying for this country, the sleeping giant to wake up and fight for our rights which are not just to be able to smoke somewhere safe or to have cheaper gas for taking trips to run away from the madness but our real rights: the right to have as many children as we might, to keep our elders with us, give them their place in our homes and a life with dignity, and a family which they have cared for all their lives and have their rights to have around. The right to speak without fear, to have a place to live without having to make Banks rich. The right to teach our children the truth and educate them with the proper correction measures, the right for our teachers to teach the dignity of men and the right to use science for the good of Humanity and to make our lives easier and not for profit and power trying to create the perfect copy of a human being instead of just accept people as they are to help them become Children of God. Yes we still have much to do and to change because to come back to the right path we need to really turn back, and stop being afraid of moving forward because "In God we Trust" should be put back not only on our money but on our homes and our school books and our Libraries and Universities and we need to believe it because it's our only hope to survive not just to say it but to trust Him all the way and if we do, He would be with us till the end of the world as He promised.

Today is the 4th of July and not only is this a very important day for all Americans but it is a very important day for me and I've always tried to celebrate it to its best. So far and since I've lived here in the States, I have celebrated it the old fashion way, either my husband cooking Barbecue meats or going as guests to enjoy the day and the Barbecue somewhere else. Why is this day so special to me? Well, first I shall say that because my husband was a soldier in the US Air Force and a very patriotic person in general, we've always celebrated this day and made sure that we will enjoy watching fireworks as a family. As a curious anecdote I shall add that one of the sisters of my Church Community was born on the 4th of July and she will make sure that the whole Community was invited to her lovely party at her parent's house where we will celebrate both her birthday and the Day of the Independence. It was a perfect arrangement and everybody had fun. After I became a widow in 1995 I've still done what I can to watch the beautiful and joyful fireworks. I used to see them at home in California and after I was sent by the Church to be an itinerant missionary I've always celebrated fireworks and all. (Itinerant means movable and ready to go anywhere that the Church might need you and leave at any time. Now that I'm an American citizen, the celebration has a lot more meaning for me and I participate more fully with the rest of the assistants to the show and I've even felt the patriotic spirit accompany us while we are together as a people during the day. When and why did I become a citizen? Well, a couple of years after my husband passed away I decided to spend Christmas with my mother in Spain and coming back at the "entrance" airport and at customs getting in, I was pointed at by a handsome, tall marine dressed on white who asked me, by name, to follow him to a small office where he offered me a chair and looking straight into my eyes what were the reasons for not had become a citizen yet and to my surprise, I gave them to him. I've told him that first off all I've didn't want to lose my Spanish citizenship of which I've always been very proud (to have), the other reason was that I've never seen the need to become an American because I enjoy all the rights and privileges as anybody else and that I've never felt any less than a citizen might feel. He listened to my reasons and then told me that I was the widow of an American soldier who had served proudly in the Air Force and maybe I should think about it to honor my husband's memory and state. I promised the marine, mostly because I needed to catch my next flight connecting to California, that I would apply for American citizenship as soon as I'd get home. After talking to family and members of my Church Community who approved of the plan, I did as I told the marine and became a proud citizen even though I hated the idea of giving up my dearest Spanish citizenship, but God had anticipated of course this development and to my surprise, in January of 2004 Spain issued a law which was called "The Law of Origen" which allowed every second generation direct descendent to apply and received the Spanish citizenship which I used immediately getting my renewed citizenship within the same year. A little sad story with a brilliant end and once more of course I'd give the credit of this fantastic turn (about) to the Mercy and splendid generosity of our God and Father in Jesus Christ.

THE COMMUNION OF SAINTS

Regarding my mental state before I joined The Church, I'm surprised that I didn't need some kind of therapy or counseling because my condition was critical and serious. I can say that now after I've been treated and still in the process of being cured but I know that Jesus Christ has cured me, transforming my sick condition and taking me little by little into sanity and normality. Society is changing rapidly and becoming more lenient regarding sexuality, morality, manners and behavior and there are fewer things which are considered wrong. Since Pornography is totally accepted, even recommended in some cases, everything is possible and "good" and that concept makes education more complicated, and I mean any type of education, even sexual (education) is becoming out of context and that is a situation where confusion takes over and clarity of thought turns obscure and diverting making people to brake basic rules. These rules set the limits to our human fragility and give us some kind of frame to act and even make the choices which would help us to decide to do the "right thing". In my case, and as The Bible says, if you confess with your mouth that Christ is the Son of God and The Saviour then you would be saved, meaning that you would be alright and that fact is the solution for most of our troubled lives. After my confession (I confess my sins to a catholic priest) my gilt was lifted from my soul, sorrow healed my wounded heart and forgiveness cleaned my mind when The Holy Spirit entered in me (The Church teaches that The Holy Spirit is present in every sacrament and acts on us as needed to receive The Grace which gives us strength) So after that experience, I changed and started to turn towards the other end of the road, literally the road to redemption and "real" happiness. The Devil can enslave us through many entries but our sexuality can be an open door and a vulnerable point which we must defend though unfortunately we leave it unprotected and since we do not know the least about these facts and do nothing, we become victims very easily, most of the time unaware of the consequences. I owe my present sanity to the message which I heard in The Church through the Catechesis that God loves me that He is The Creator that Jesus took my place on the cross and gave His live for me and suffered for me so that I could do the same and also suffer for the other which it's the second rule or Commandment to live Life as it should be lived.

That is why the Pope's book "The Sexuality of The Body" gives the answers that we need to change the wrongs into rights, to remedy all our mistakes and to be able to tell others (particularly young people) to stay away from the lies of the evil one. Lies which will make us think wrong thoughts and to do the wrong thing. Simplicity as The Church teaches is good advice and complicated things are better off away from us. I hope that through my experience I can also help others not to be victims but victorious in Jesus Christ!

Of how The Lord, through His Word (Jesus) has been changing my ways, my habits, my way of thinking and reacting and even points of my personality and I am happier now that I have ever been because The Church, the Holy Spirit guidance, is recreating in me a new person in every aspect of my life. When I was a young beautiful woman I was a flirt because I was sick with all kinds of traumas and defects and in front of any difficult event I would react violently and always looking for a way out to my satisfaction which never came as I wanted it. The here and now was a necessity and for the little that I can remember, I was wrong most of the time. Those results would drive me mad and I've given up to my frustration which led me to negative thoughts. That was me more or less half of a century ago because I started to go out with my friends (without the knowledge of my mother) as soon as I left the catholic school where my sister and I went to get an education. So by the time I was in my sweet 16 years, I already had a few admirers and pretty soon I experienced the power that I had (as a woman) over a man. The discovery created in me a passion for flirting which I would discover only years later and, after my first confession since I have been in school, I've realized the need I had to get love and attention at any price; the love and attention which I didn't get from my father (according to my subconscious) I liked the company of men in general and I would look for them any place I could. Later on, thanks to the guidance and enlightenment of Mother Church, I could see how sick I was and how this deceiving passion had marked my soul from a very young age. I became a mature woman and left my home to travel to London to learn the English language according to me but once in that country and even though I learnt the language, my main interest was men again and I attracted the attention of a young Slovak man who became my first sexual encounter. The relationship didn't progress due to poor communication skills and also the fact that I wasn't ready to work at any serious mature relationship. I was always looking for adventure and instant gratification because of my illness and after I left England without even explaining myself to him, I immediately met my future husband. The Slovak who was a gentlemen, came to Spain in pursuit of his "girlfriend" and since my sister who was still in England, has provided him with my address and telephone number, he contacted me and wanted to see me. I was already going steady with Carl my husband because as I said before, we only courted for a short time. Anyhow, he met with the both of us and we talked and of course, he realized that I wasn't going to be his girlfriend any longer. The encounter was romantic but my boyfriend was upset because he didn't understand what was going on between us. He was a real gentleman, both of them and I was fortunate that nobody caused any trouble. Wenceslaus, that was his name, went back to England and later on married an adorable English girl and moved to Australia.

Last night on Shabat (comes from Sabado) or Sabado comes from Shabat my Church Community celebrated the Eucharist (Sunday Mass) together as a Memorial to honor our sister Rosa Nelly Galiano who passed away early in the morning on the same day. Her death was so close to Sunday that we all felt that she had been taken as a Sunday offering to The Lord. I know it might feel like a pagan ritual but for a Christian, we are all (as the Body of Christ) called to be an offering together, with His Son who is The Head. I don't know if I'm making any sense but I think that this the best that I can explain this liturgical mystery and I also know that The Catholic Church has been accused many times of keeping mysteries and dark secrets hidden from the rest of Humanity but the fact is that The Church's mystery has and it is being revealed to us from its beginnings and Christians should and must know that the last book of the Bible is called Revelation and everything that has happened and that it would happen it's been written there. But don't take my word for it; investigate the scriptures, ask the Church, read its many documents, use enough time to study and acquire all the knowledge that we need and that it is there for us. "Investigate the Scriptures" Shouts St. Paul in the noisy Synagogues of Judea because he knew how important it is to learn our history, our past and by following the prophets, we can also see our future, but we need to study seriously and continually to reach the kind of wisdom necessary in our lives and in the lives of our fellow men. Last night during the Eucharist, we prayed for the soul of our sister Rosa Nelly to reach Heaven as soon as possible because we know how much she suffered and how much she cried to The Lord to have mercy on her and for His will to be done on her. That is an action and a position that we can get only through a deep faith and by embracing the cross which God allows in every moment of our lives. We pray to The Lord to have mercy on her soul and also to help her family to endure this painful event. Both her daughters were in the Assembly, her sister and brother in law were also present. I believed that she had a small number of close relatives because most of the family lives in Colombia and couldn't make it to the United States in time.

The celebration was lovely, intimate and tender, very tender. We sang Church songs which were adequate for the occasion and I notice tears running from the faces of some of the people present. The readings mention the communion of The Church being present in our hour of need and we also remember her last words to us and the courage that she showed till her last minute. The presence of the Church by her bed was a sign of brotherly hood mentioned in the Scriptures many times and to visit and comfort the sick is one of the Works of Mercy proclaimed and accepted by The Catholic Church as actions inspired for Her to receive the graces which are necessary because The Church has been called by the Vatican II Council, The Sacrament of Salvation for The World. Our sister Rosa Nelly would be taken care of, we would honor her departure as the beginning of her new life as we had been taught that she is alive and that her soul should never die but go back to its source which is divine and eternal. The Church these days will send her to The Father to joint the Communion of Saints which is one of the articles of The Creed. She would also be blessed, prepared and bury in Christian soil in the presence of the official Church, the Assembly and the Priest who would be presiding representing Christ. Rosa Nelly pray for us!

Today Saturday, September 24, 2011 one of my Church sisters (sister in Christ) has passed away early this morning. Her name was Rosa Nelly (Manuela?) She has been born in Colombia, a single mother of two beautiful young ladies. Her passing wasn't a surprise for me, even though death always is, because I have been to visit her at the hospital in Hackensack last Tuesday. We prayed Morning Prayer (Lauds) and talked about different things and memories and it was all together a very nice and meaningful visit. She was cheerful and loving and she would mention from time to time that she was open to the Will of God, which is an unusual comment for a person who is receiving Chemotherapy and Radiation almost daily as her treatment for spinal cancer. My sister in Christ Rosa, has been fighting this devastated illness for years and when I've met her, two years ago, she was already sick. Her attitude has always been positive and I remember her telling me that when you are being treated for cancer, your positive approach to the illness would meant a tremendous difference and your mental and spiritual situation has a lot to do with the process of healing that you are undergoing, wherever it might be. Her comments called my attention and I accepted this being a good approach to getting well or, at least, to be in a state of understanding and acceptance necessary for the battle going on in your body and involving of course your mind. As a matter of fact, her comments helped me very much when I was in the hospital recently having an implant of the "Mitral valve" which is located in the center of the heart. In the most difficult moments, I would remember her words and it meant a difference in my attitude which resulted in a more readiness to the healing process. Now as she passes to the Father, I feel that she has made a difference in my live and in the way to recovery and I am thankful for her insight and the sharing of her experience with me. The Church teaches that death is a step, a passing and that even though the body suffers a terrible fear of separation from the soul and from the reality which it knows, it is a natural process and we all are to go through it and there is nothing we can do about it but, The Church also teaches that Jesus Christ the Son of God, and the Second Person of the Holy Trinity was sent, as agreed, to live with us, share our Humanity and give his life to redeem (rescue) us. Because of this fact, and being the Son of God, he conquered death and made it fearless showing us, through His Resurrection, that death wasn't the end but that it is the door to real Life and to Heaven. I was making a comment to another of my sisters in Christ regarding this and I said that there is one way (road) in life and we choose to go left or right or if you must go up and down but we wouldn't stay in just one place. Either we move forward towards Good or God's Will or we follow evil and it's ways and do His will and by choosing what side to take we find the fulfillment of our free will. Now The Church asks us to obey the commandments, to receive the Sacraments and to follow Jesus Christ till the end even to give our lives for this purpose and if we do it willingly we have found happiness as its best. To do otherwise would mean the beginning of our fall down and the loss of our souls which are looking for The Creator. May He deals mercifully with my sister Rosa Nelly during her passing towards Eternity and her soul to reach Heaven as its final goal. Amen

Philly, PA 09/24/2015

Yes, We're passing by in "enemy territory" Life is a combat and Christians must be disposed to combat to the death. How? By being prepared with the shield of Faith together with the armor of God. By receiving the Spirit of Jesus who has chosen to go to the cross for us. God, the Father have chosen the whole scenario, the Roman Empire, The Jew Nation under their power, etc. Romans used this horrible instrument of torture which would produce a painful death at the end, but He did not open His mouth but suffered everything for us, so that we would be free.

He has been preparing for this mission. Mary, his mother, a true daughter of Israel from birth, had also been prepared for this mission, the perfect plan of salvation. For those who have faith, the Christians, -chosen from baptism- are called and prepared for a similar mission also, and share this with others.

St. Agustin says: "If we cannot have the catechumenate beforehand, we'll carry it out afterwards, that is, the instruction, completion and education, the whole of the Church's educative work, after baptism.

The sacrament of Christian regeneration must once again return to being what it was in the consciousness and customs of the first norms of the first generation of Christians. (from the catequesis of Pope Paul VI)

Union City NJ 0/27/2012

Dear Ms Joan, What is the government's role? Do you honestly know the answer? Is the Constitution still the clear and fair document that our forefathers signed to protect us from all the terrible events that we have experienced during these last decades? Where is the American Way of Life?...the Good Life? Is it forever gone? Or can we still hold on to it even for a while longer? My experience is this: YES! If we could be still for a moment and let go of some bad choices and bring back the good ones. "Mitt" as you call him, didn't forget the government's role because he is a law abiding citizen who has done very well for himself and what's wrong with that? That IS the American Way. To go to college, to study, to be a good citizen and work hard and obey the law (which we the people made) and become independent and rich? If you could? Yes I'd say, that is the American Way...the American Dream and we are supposed to pass it on to others even until the next generation of Americans. I believe that what Mitt is doing is a very proper thing (as the British would say) Is he to be concerned for the very poor right now? No because they're well cared for (and that is also the American Way). He is concerned about the general welfare, the people that can vote and put him in office and, from there, he "Mitt" may be able (with the support of the People ") to manage the country and bring it back to its original state. A country for ALL rich and poor, to live, not as "victims' ' depending on the will of the government, but as healthy, free, well fed citizens, strong enough to govern and not just to be governed. You were right when you said that "most Americans tithe to their faith and donate to charity" and those are the Americans that, like "Mitt" are "well enough" to do it. Good day to you.

Philly, PA 09/24/2015

Yes, We're passing by in "enemy territory" Life is a combat and Christians must be disposed to combat to the death. How? By being prepared with the shield of Faith together with the armor of God. By receiving the Spirit of Jesus who has chosen to go to the cross for us. God, the Father have chosen the whole scenario, the Roman Empire, The Jew Nation under their power, etc. Romans used this horrible instrument of torture which would produce a painful death at the end, but He did not open His mouth but suffered everything for us, so that we would be free.

He has been preparing for this mission. Mary, his mother, a true daughter of Israel from birth, had also been prepared for this mission, the perfect plan of salvation. For those who have faith, the Christians, -chosen from baptism- are called and prepared for a similar mission also, and share this with others.

Envy is the only deadly sin in which there is no pleasure nor any gratification, and it has the unenviable feature that it only produces sadness. Writer Nancy Kennedy calls the feeling "ugly" "It gets in the face of God and says: All that you have graciously provided me all my life is not enough!"

I grew up a Catholic (Our home in Canary Islands was only a couple of blocks from the parish) . My mom would dress us up in our Sunday clothes and send the younger children, in charge of the oldest, Juan Francisco to Mass. According to what she'd tell us, she has also been educated in the Catholic Faith though her father "Grandpa" was an idealist who's political tendencies has taken him away from Church since his youth. My memories of him were about a well dressed gentleman family loving and his own ideas about life and morals. He and my grandmother would visit us as often as his duties would permit him to. His name John has been passed on to some of the male members of the family, among them, one of my sons. After my father Francisco-Leon passed away, my mother sold my father's business to his associate and friend. She also sold the furniture and took us all on a ship back to my grandmother in Madrid. I was already a teen and understood living the islands behind as, once my father was out of the picture, our place was back with her side of the family. I still think that it was a good move since all of us benefited from a life at the capital where, not only we received the support of the family there, but got a better and broader education as well.

We lived in a comfortable flat in a stable and well known neighborhood right in front of the beautiful park called El Retiro, where my brothers and sisters met new friends and played, whether permitted. There in this park I met the son of an actor and that made me feel very important. We stayed at my grandmother's place for some time until Franco decided to provide apartments for widows with more than 3 children and whose husbands had been involved in the right side of the Civil War.

Soon some of us were sent off to Catholic Schools where we continued our education. My younger sister Angela and I went to the same school, one of my brothers went to a boarding school on the

Sierra near Madrid and my older brother and sister attended a school nearby. Ana, the baby, only 2 or 3 years of age, remained at home.

Something interesting is that my older sister Elizabeth (named after my mother and grandmother) before she passed away, decided to visit the islands and paid her respects to my father by taking flowers to the tomb and cleaning the tombstone. After this was done, she took pictures to show them to us. I've appreciated this moving thought.

Philly 09/11/2015

About questions and answers to Life: Before I left Carl (my husband) I had something on my mind "I want I must be happy!" I would tell myself once and again; 'If I was to die today or tomorrow, what would I like to be doing? How would I like to be living? Those were the questions that I had to answer. And this was, "I need to be happy, to leave the life that I was living and for that, I must run away, leave Carl who made me So unhappy and maybe find someone else. I have the right to be happy! I said to myself" "The pursuit of Happiness" that is the meaning of the culture of this country The U.S.A That made perfect sense to me in those days. It's part of my past now. Somehow I knew that I needed to find happiness, to feel good! Those were my thoughts and I acted on them. First thing, get out of here and go to Spain back to my family where I've always felt wanted and loved. I have been with my alcoholic, abusive husband for almost 8 years (I thought of the famous (7 year itch) Seven difficult and exhausting years. I chose to change, to give myself another chance. I know now that I didn't know what I was doing. I have been very much influenced by the "feminist movement" so popular and powerful during those years, "Women are free" "We can do wherever We want with our bodies" etc. You already know the rest of the story.

Philly 09/15/2015

We all come from somewhere, right? We're going somewhere. Life is a mystery too important, too precious to be just a daily routine being lived just because we have to. If that is so, why take your life? What is the hurry? How can we take it anymore? Why so many babies? Schools, what is the use of so many hospitals, doctors, medicines, how come some are rich, some are poor, why do we need to have money and lots of it? There must be a good reason to live, to be born, to be here at this exactly time and society, to fall in love, to marry, travel, visit relatives, to want to have children or not to have them, to love, to have friends, to explain our situation to others, to eat 3 or 4 times a day (depending the country where we are eating, chose between drinking coffee or tea, why do the English prefer tea to any other hot drink, even though now there is Coca Cola in their country, why is the Mediterranean diet different and considered healthy, why do the Europeans drink wine? Etc... There have to be reasons for men to choose different types of food, drinks, even air lines. Why the fear of death? In our recent society, we would rather kill someone and still their organs than accept to die. Why? There has to be something marvelous, extraordinary, tremendous, extremely important that keeps us wanting to live. If that is so, let's get to it! Search, "ask and it shall be given to you" says The Lord, the Church.

Why did I married and to a beautiful person as Carl was, he was catholic, not that catholics are perfect saint not even perfect people but what I means is that we at the time we meet, were baptized and members of the same church, both educated in Catholic schools and both received the needed sacraments to be able to receive the sacrament of marriage in the same church. What I'm questioning myself about is…that had God planned for Ray to be the father of my two sons and therefore the grandfather of all our grandchildren? I know that God is in charge and nothing can be done (good or bad) without His consent. My yes to Carl was the beginning of a new life. Even though he was a descendent of Spaniards knew the Spanish language and culture and has been educated in the Catholic fashion and faith, he was still far from the church and very much in the ways of the world. I knew that he was involved in relations with other women, but it was different between us; there was a tenderness and affection from the moment that we met and, since he and my sister were friends, the feeling of trust was mutual and we fell in love.

Our survival instincts are fierce, powerful and ready to fight. They are extraordinarily well coordinated and to the point and it is a matter of life and death being given to us creatures as a gift and not as a curse which is what some areas of society might believe. I experienced this when I was in the hospital to have a heart valve implant and because the surgery had complications, my life was in danger and I knew it. Thanks to the power and graces which come from prayer, I cling to life as a shell to the rock and my desire to live was stronger than the delicate state of my health. How I experienced such a formidable will power to survive is beyond my knowledge of the human body but I know now what the power of prayer and the support of the Spiritual Body of Christ can achieve in a moment of extreme suffering and distress. I also prayed together with different members of the Church Community where I belong and my prayer was honest and sincere and I begged God to allow me more time because I wasn't ready to die. I remember my prayer and what I said was that I knew that If I die during that time, I will surely go to Hell because I am a sinner and even in that moment of distress and serious danger, I didn't felt any contrition for my many sins and, because of that fact, I wasn't ready to start the journey towards Eternity. Those hundreds of sincere prayers made an enormous difference in my struggle with death and Hope took over as it should be because it is a virtue and it (Hope) has an orderly process that brings it to the needy person before he loses his peace and enters into the disturbance of despair. In general, in those moments humans look for relief and turn to science for solutions but, when science fails…what can we do? I turned to God, thanks to the faith of the Church and It's support and this Unity and strength would act as a shield against the attacks of the evil one who would destroy us if given the chance. I still feel, sometimes, into doubt and while I think of the implant, I enter into despair and sadness but only for a moment because the will of God is stronger than mine and in those moments I turn to Him and beg Him for help. When I do that, as a grace, I immediately experience peace of mind and the shadow of my dark thoughts disappear. So there is life after death and there is health and acceptance in the most terrible illness and our more difficult situations because Jesus conquered death and opened Heaven for us, all of us. That is the reason for our Hope and that invisible step which we can go down to when the abyss appears open in front of us, wide and dark like a ferocious, scary dragon. Yes, death is ferocious and scary but someone conquered it, made it weak, losing its fierceness and making it possible for The Day After to have true meaning again. The Resurrection of Christ is an extraordinary event which changed the course of History and because of it, Humanity was made anew and given a Destiny. I know that these words might look to you like a Hollywood science movie but, behind them, there is the perfect plan of The Creator, the one who created the Universe and everything in it, is Eternal and, therefore, life is Eternal also and never ending because Life is God.

Today it (is) a Saturday and I'm getting ready to go to a Presbytery Ordination which is a Liturgical Ceremony presided by the local Bishop, where the candidates who have been approved and fund worthy to take the next step are to be ordain priests even though the word Presbyter is more appropriate since all the members of the Universal Church (the one known as Catholic) are called and prepared to be and live as Priests. This is an interesting concept which many Catholics ignore or simply do not have knowledge of it. I've learned it while being prepared to accept and recognize my Baptism walking in The Way or Catecumenado which is called neo- to identify the fact that the candidates (or those called to belong to it) have already been baptized and are only reliving or rediscovering this important Sacrament. The beginning of Christian Life or the consecration to the service of God. That is why it is important as a baptized member to remain in the Church and frequent its Liturgies and religious services to receive at times the many Graces which the Holy Spirit would spread about us. Precisely, fifty days after Easter or the Passover Vigil, there is the Feast called Pentecost (Pente) meaning fifty and during this Church gathering we, the members gathered, could receive if found in the appropriate state of mind and body, the gifts of the Spirit liturgical known as The Paraclete. A priest friend of mine welcomed me to a Eucharist which he was presiding over with the words: from Feast to Feast (de Fiesta en Fiesta) because that is how he saw my frequent visits to celebrations during different seasons of the Church Calendar Year. I've always been ready to go to any important Church Event where I'm invited because I know the One who invites is The Lord and His passing means Graces for me. I know that for some people that could be a sign of being kind of fanatic but Life is short and I cannot miss a Church gathering where The Holy Spirit could be present and, because of it, my life could change and I would receive a New Spirit. Today I've been in a Presbytery Ordination as I was saying above where 18 candidates had been ordained and I happen to know four of them and I have been invited by two of the candidates. I went to the magnificent Cathedral of Newark and took my sit to enjoy the beautiful celebration of the Ordination which lasted 2 hours or more but it was worth it. After Church we, the sister from my community who was driving me, her husband and I, went to the restaurant where the meal (a banquet) was ready and the party began. Beautiful antipasto dishes, good, rich Italian wines, desserts, all this accompanied by Italian liquors and Espresso coffee. The new priest sang old Italian songs and some of the guests also joined the singing and entertainment. All together a wonderful day in the company of brothers and sisters from the new priest's church community, relatives and friends who have come from Italy to be with him. My sister, her husband and I had a great time and I'm looking forward to the next presbyter's order...... Salute to the new priests!!! God Bless you.

I don't know how to explain myself clearly or I should say clearer than it comes from my mind and this is something that had interfered with the way that I express my thoughts, feelings and sentiments, in other words, to use language to be, to say, to use my personal power, by being an individual completed different to any other person; one unique creation and that is why denying Creation, the act of being created eliminates the meaning of life, the reason of living. Being alive, said somebody I know, is not just to have a beating pulse, a working brain and blood running through our veins, no. Being alive is to remain alive even after your body does not respond to the signs of life which have been accepted by the general opinion on science, physics and any other order of authority that society has known as official rules of life or death. It is interesting to observe medical personal treating their patients as if they were experimenting and/or learning to see how a certain treatment acts on a particular moment and for a possible more or less known illness in a particular person and this is what I've experienced after being taken to the hospital suffering a bad case of heart trouble. My heart needed an implant; one of the valves was damaged and that was, according to several cardiologists, the only solution for my condition which was serious. This unwelcome episode happened the day after Thanksgiving of 2011 and I had surgery to correct the problem a few weeks later on March the first, a date which I thought was very adequate for such repair. Eleven days later and after going through one of the most dangerous experiences of my, I think, long life, the surgeon came to my room to see me and to ask me when I wanted to go home. His question made me the happiest that I have been since this illness disrupted the quiet order of my daily routine, forcing me to enter into the type of hell that I would've ever imagined. Ever since I was taken to the hospital, I knew that I had to give my life and time to God because only by putting Him first and giving up most of my free choices during this time, I would encounter His Grace. I only did it with His help and His mercy, experiencing every day His presence and strength. My son the priest came to keep me company making sure that I would have the best of care and the professional attention was needed at such a delicate healing process and, even though the treatment (it) was tough I received it with gladness and a thankful attitude that somehow impressed the hospital personnel to the point that some of the nurses and technicians would come to see me just because of curiosity. Getting out of the hospital alive represented a wellness inside that I wouldn't have expected and my first meal that day cooked by one of the sisters of my Church Community tasted like food from Heaven itself.

Today is Friday of the month of May and a beautiful spring day, golden clouds surrounded by soft sun rays which makes everything serene and right. On this day we had the Bishop's visit in St. Anthony of Padua parish because he'd confirmed a group of candidates for the sacrament of Confirmation. One of the candidates is an adult who belongs to one of the communities at the parish and has been prepared to receive the Sacrament for some time. I was waiting outside St. Anthony's standing in the corner getting ready to walk home after an exciting and exhausting meal which I've prepared for the Bishop, his companion, the two priests from the parish and the official cat…… who helped prepared the classes for the candidates to receive this important Sacrament; finally there was also a deacon who is to be ordained presbyter very soon. All together a very memorable reunion and, according to the guests at table, a very well done "paella". I was tired but satisfied with the success of my meal and that is one of the reasons why I felt so good waiting outside the parish looking at the golden clouds and thanking God for helping me to do it right. My two roommates who are also missionaries helped me to set the table, serve and pick up and one of the sisters of my community in West N.Y. came over also to serve. So I was feeling pretty thankful and started walking home where my cat…. A widow from California, was waiting for her dinner. The walk was nice and it helped me to relax after the stress of organizing and preparing to receive the Bishop and his guests. I think of my past and the life that I used to live and I can't help to compare with the life that I am living now. The feeling of thankfulness towards God comes up from my heart and my soul rejoices for the Graces that I received when He called me back to His church and forgave me of all my sins which gave me the impulse to change my views about everything and the way that I used to think and act before. So I arrived at the apartment that I shared with the two missionary women which I've mentioned and dinner was already served which made me feel double blessed and more thankful if possible. This day is almost over and I still have the energy to sit and write this page even though I know that I should rest because tomorrow we are going to N.Y. and it there will be a lot of seeing and walking but I still have the same feeling of thankfulness that I started feeling at the beginning of the day and that is another Miracle for me.

I became a widow in 1995. In the same year, the three men in my life left the house. First Christopher our first born got married to a beautiful California girl who is also a member of our Church Community. They were married during the month of April; My husband Carl passed away on the last day of July and the baby Michael went first to Rome to be sent to a seminary in September. I found myself alone for the first time in my life and somehow the house seemed bigger than when we were all together. I remember that that month of July we went to Spain on vacation but of course only my husband and I and Michael. Carl wanted to go and say his goodbyes to my family and to see the country which he loved for the last time. I knew that he was very sick and weak and tried to dissuade him from taking such a long trip but there was no use and off we went. Most of the time he would be on his own, walking or having a drink here and there. He would have loved to be with my brother in law Jorge and he had a very good time anyway. We came back home to California just in time for him to prepare to die because that is exactly what he did. One week after we arrived from Spain, he told me that he wasn't feeling well and I asked him if he wanted me to take him to the hospital. He will always go to the veteran's hospital and it was near the house, but he asked me not to take him. As I saw him getting worse, I asked him if he would let Christopher take him; he said yes and he drove him over. He would not come home again and he died the following Sunday afternoon as all of us spent the day in a Church retreat with our community. That day the community decided to try to finish early to go to the hospital to visit him and we did but when we arrived at the hospital the doctor approached us to tell us that he was sorry but my husband was dead, he tried to bring him back with the help of electro shocks but to no avail. He was ready to go and went peacefully according to the doctor's explanation. The first thing I said to him was: that he had done everything he could and no to be sorry because it was his time to go. He gave me a rare look and slowly walked away. I don't remember crying right away but praying and the brothers and sisters started praying with me. My sons were crying I think and my daughter in law Marisol, now four months pregnant, was trying to console me and hugged me. The hospital personnel were somehow surprised to see us all there praying and accepting his death well but they didn't know that we had been praying all day asking God the Father to have mercy on him and help him go to Him. To believe in Eternal Life is a gift of the Holy Spirit, there is no going around it or trying to think that it is true. Either you believe it or you don't and only The Church has the key to open the great treasure of Faith without which none of us can accept death. In the Gospel of S. John (The Bible Jn 10:14) the expression "to know" does not mean a pure intellectual activity but an experience, a presence which ends up necessarily in being in Love. In Christianity we experience death and also The Resurrection which comes right after and that is an important difference.

If being a Christian becomes difficult or easy it is up to you. God make a covenant with the people of Israel, (Ex 34:27) which was chosen by Him because of its heritage and the fact that this Nation, Israel (all the twelve tribes) had been enslaved by Egypt a country which has befriended the family of Joseph one of the sons of Jacob, son of Isaac, son of Abraham the father of Faith who was a friend of God, a very close friend. (Gn 12:1-3) As History tells, after Faraon the friend of the Hebrews has passed away, the friendship cooled off for economic reasons. Because (of) the extraordinary number of workers needed for the construction of the Pyramids and other gigantic stone monuments which were so desirable to the Egyptians, one of the later Pharos disposed of his former guests and made them work for him and for the country. According to the Scriptures the work was unbearable, the treatment inhuman and the hit, the hunger, the abuses, lack of basic necessities and of course the loss of their identity as a Nation, exhausted their patience and these people stopped being happy but always claimed to their God, Yahweh and because of this devotion and fidelity, God listened to them and send them a Savior, Moses. (Ex 3:9-10) I think you know the rest of the story also you could read The Bible or watch the 10 Commandments because that's is not the point even though to know The Bible is very important to receive from The Church the revelation of the scriptures and the fear of The Lord is the beginning of Wisdom says the Word.

( ) As I was saying, if being and remaining a Christian becomes difficult or servile is because you have become difficult or servile or something else, but Christian and I said this convinced that God made a covenant with us who are still the remnant of Jacob His chosen people, Israel. And if God made the Covenant (Gn 15:1) He will keep it forever and not make it hard for us or boring or impossible to follow. He will keep His part and our part and His fire will devour both sides of the animals laying open on the stones their halves exposed to the consuming fire according to the ancient way to fulfill this popular ritual. (Gn 15:1) If He does His part and ours, where is the difficulty? Where is the impossibility? Everything is possible for the one that waits in The Lord

( ) My experience for now is to open my mouth and He would fill it; make a step closer and He would take your hand, run a tear and He would keep it in a vase and use that tear to add it to the sufferings of His son on the cross. Lift your eyes to Heaven and He would send His Spirit over your head. This is a God of mercy and forgiveness, our Father as we said while praying the Our Father the prayer that Jesus Himself thought His disciples and they thought it to us The Church. Our part is to follow Jesus who is The Way to Heaven but we must first follow Him through the streets of Jerusalem up Calvary (Colgotta) and walk the way to meekness and obedience and said yes to His plan for you and carry your cross and follow () as He tells us. That is why He did it first and opened the way for us so that we can walk with Him. To be a Christian is not that difficult is to transform from the first man (Adam) into the new man (Jesus) live the old man in the waters of Baptism and receive the new one while coming out of the waters (representing death) going up the steps which it is the catechumenate and becoming a new creation the new creature with the same spirit of Jesus Christ and, according to the Scriptures, capable of performing jet greater deeds.( ).

ENDNOTES

<u>1</u> * Preach the Gospel through catequesis (catechesis) the history of salvation beginning from the Patriarch Abraham to our days and the role of humanity (all of us) in such ???. I'll explain in another chapter.

www.ingramcontent.com/pod-product-compliance
Lightning Source LLC
LaVergne TN
LVHW011935070526
838202LV00054B/4652